True Crime

Aileen Wuornos

The Horrifying Story of the Female

Serial Killer that Terrorized Humanity

Ryan James

TABLE OF CONTENTS

Chapter One: The History 1

Chapter Two: Florida Living 12

Chapter Three: The Lesbians 22

Chapter Four: Damsel of Death 33

Chapter Five: End of the Road 44

Chapter Six: Friends or Foes? 55

Chapter Seven: A Feminist's Analysis 66

Chapter Eight: Case Examination 77

Chapter Nine: In Her Own Words 90

Chapter Ten: In Closing 102

Chapter One

The History

A woman some call "The Damsel of Death" or "The Highway Hooker" was executed on October 9, 2002 for her killings of seven Florida men over the course of one year. She has claimed to have killed one other man, but that can't be accounted for because his body was never found. Wuornos claimed that all seven of her victims had either tried to rape her, torture her, or kill her, and while it is believed that her first victim, Richard Charles Mallory, had in fact tried to rape and torture her, the rest of her claims were quickly proven to be false. Wuornos was very vicious with her attacks. Shooting each victim several times at point-blank range, and later stealing their cars and belongings before she dumped their bodies and sped off into the night.

Aileen Lee Wuornos, born Aileen Carol Pittman, is oftentimes referred to as the first female serial killer. Of course, she isn't, because women have been killing since long before she was born. However, Wuornos earned her title strictly based on her violent nature. Most female killers choose victims that are close to them, whereas Aileen chose strangers. Other female killers tend to stick to using poisons as their weapon, whereas Aileen chose a gun and shot her victims multiple times. Before she was executed in a Florida state prison, Aileen Wuornos reigned terror on all of Florida's highways, and this is her story.

The woman known to the world for her hatred of all humans, was born in Troy, Michigan on February 29, 1956. Her mother, Diane Wuornos and her father, Leo Dale Pittman, were still children themselves when they got married and started a family. When Aileen was just four years old, her mother gave up on being a single mother and abandoned her and her older brother Keith at the front steps of their grandparents. Who later legally adopted them both. She was never able to meet her real dad because he was locked up long before she was born, and she had forgotten all about her birth mother at such a young age.

She and Keith were under the impression that their grandparents were their real parents for the longest time. It wasn't until Aileen had discovered they were adopted, at about twelve years old, that she started to rebel. Not only that, but her grandfather was abusive to her.

2

Physically, sexually, mentally, and emotionally. Lauri and Britta Wuornos were both severe alcoholics who struggled with raising their own two children, on top of Aileen and Keith. It isn't often talked about, but Aileen and Keith were raised with their aunt and uncle—as their brother and sister.

As if that alone wasn't troubling enough, Aileen's grandfather had started to molest her when she was just shy of eleven years old. The old man had a terrible temper, much like his granddaughters. That, along with his heavy drinking and strictness on her and her brother, made it nearly impossible for the two of them to get along. She sought help from her grandmother, but the woman was too afraid of her husband. Not wanting to go against his hand, she did her best to keep Aileen out of his way.

Given her upbringing, it isn't hard to imagine a young Aileen being sexually promiscuous. She has even gone on record to state that she and Keith had sex with each other at times. A family friend has also confirmed that to be true. Her role as a prostitute began at around the same age. She started out selling her body to the boys at school and around the neighborhood for small things like cigarettes, booze, and food. She also made her rounds to scrape up enough cash to throw parties in the woods, as a way to gain herself more friends. She was never really popular with the other kids at school. Most of them were afraid of her because of her explosive temper and the way she lashed out on everyone.

By age fourteen, Aileen had gotten pregnant. Her grandparents didn't find out until she was about six months in, that's how little attention was paid to her and Keith. It was always unclear who the father was, but rumor has it, Aileen had either been molested by a friend of her grandfather's, or she let herself become willingly involved with him and he had gotten her pregnant. Nonetheless, her grandfather immediately made arrangements for the child to be adopted the minute Aileen gave birth. He shipped her off to a place called "The House for Unwed Mothers" where Aileen spent the next nine months locked away from the life she knew back home in Troy. She was in no way capable of caring for a baby. She was just a baby herself, and with her undiagnosed mental illnesses and explosive temper, her baby boy would have been nothing more than a hinder to her life, as well as her grandparents. Either that, or she would have ended up killing him because she couldn't handle the responsibilities that came along with motherhood.

When she returned home from The House for Unwed Mothers, Aileen's grandmother died not long after her return. The old woman's liver had finally given out on her due to her heavy drinking. Her grandfather blamed Aileen and Keith for his wife's death. The old man claimed that the two of them put too much stress on their grandmother. Diane, Aileen's birth mother, believed that her father actually killed his wife, though there were never any signs of foul play.

With all of the bullying Aileen endured after returning to school from giving birth, and the death of her grandmother, she decided to drop out at age fifteen. She had had enough. Her grandmother and her brother Keith were the only lights she had in her life. But, with Keith often running away from home to stay with friends in the neighborhood, looking to escape the wrath of their grandfather, and her grandmother dead and gone, Aileen was left alone to catch the backlash. When she finally started running away with Keith and her grandfather no longer had access to her, sexually, he grew even more furious with her and kicked her out on the streets.

Dawn Botkins, Aileen's best friend from school, kept her company a lot of the time. They slept in abandoned cars together and hit the local parties to escape their hell of a reality. Aileen even slept in the woods most nights because she had nowhere else to go. She and Keith still kept in contact, but he was also a straggler, so he had no means of giving her a place to stay. By age sixteen, Aileen hit the road heading west. She hitchhiked the entire way, using her good looks and selling her body to make a way for herself.

It's hard to say whether or not Aileen took after her birth mother in any way, whereas on the other hand, it's very easy to see the traits she picked up from her real father. Her grandfather as well. Leo Dale Pittman, a spoiled brat being raised by his grandparents as well. When his grandfather died, his grandmother continued to spoil him and aid in his rotten behavior. You could easily argue that the woman was afraid of her grandson, as he was often mean and physically abusive to her and their animals. Leo had been diagnosed with schizophrenia early on in life and was later labeled a "career criminal" for his string of petty crimes, and an even bigger crime that landed him a life sentence behind bars: the kidnapping and rape of a seven-year-old girl. Pittman was also the main suspect in the murder of another young girl. To avoid having to serve his life sentence, Pittman hung himself in his cell.

Diane and Leo had a terrible marriage. There was a lot of violence, on Leo's part. His mental illness played a major role in that for the both of them. They eloped when Diane was just fourteen years old, and Leo was sixteen. Diane left home at a young age because of her father's strictness and her love for Leo. He was a bad boy who really struck her interest. Of course her father and mother weren't very fond of their daughter dating at such a young age, but that didn't stop her. Diane regretted her decision to marry Leo. He was abusive, schizophrenic, and also a child molester. Their marriage only lasted about two years before Diane filed for a divorce. After his first run-in with the law, Leo was allowed to enlist in the military, to avoid doing jail time. That was when Diane seized her moment of freedom. While he was away she learned that being a single parent of two young children was hard. She wasn't cut out to care for children on her own, so she dropped the children off at her parents and disappeared.

Aileen had been abandoned her entire life. Those feelings haunted her all the way up to adulthood, leading her down a dark path of petty crimes like theft and prostitution, and eventually murder. There was a lot missing and a lot wrong with Aileen. Most people like to believe the reasons for her murdering seven, possibly eight men, was that she simply hated men. But, that wasn't the case. Aileen hated people in general. While incarcerated she had been diagnosed with borderline personality disorder, PTSD, and anti-socialism. Researchers believe her mental illness had been passed down from her father, while others believe she got it honestly from both sides. She's often labeled as strange, rebellious, and ignorant. Even the police say it wasn't hard to find her guilty because of her many outbursts and almost proud-like demeanor towards her crimes. She sealed her own fate in the way she bragged and boasted while being interrogated. Claiming all seven men raped her was the lick that sealed the deal for investigators.

To say that Aileen was destined for a life of crime would be an understatement. She never stood a chance at life from the very beginning. Was she born to kill? That is a question that arises often, when talking about the late Aileen Lee Wuornos. A lot of people, women in particular, go through life experiencing the same types of environments and abuse that Aileen had, however, not all of them become serial killers. In fact, not all of them commit any crimes at all. For Aileen, life was different. Very different. She was a ticking time bomb of a human being, searching for love and softness anywhere she could, but never found it. Mostly because of her own behavior and belligerent outbursts. No one could deal with her, not even herself at times. It had always been suspected that Aileen took after her father when it came to her mental health, yet and still, no one had ever taken the time out to actually get her seen by doctors. Some say it wouldn't have mattered either way. Aileen was a bad seed and needed to be put down. She's even stated that herself throughout her trial. "You have to kill Aileen Wuornos. Because I will kill again," she said.

Though, in the state of Florida, a death warrant cannot be issued for those who aren't mentally fit to stand trial, Jeb Bush agreed with Wuornos and signed the death warrant himself. Aileen had undergone several psych evaluations and was determined to understand the extent of her crimes, as well as her punishment. In fact, she actually pushed for the death penalty. She wanted to die. She stated that she refused to live her life behind bars, so they could either kill her and get it over with, or she would do it herself. Much like her father. Once her sentence was handed down to her, six life terms, she even stopped going to appeal meetings. That was just how much she wanted her life to end. At one point during her trial, Aileen fired her public defender because she wanted her to make a deal of death and the woman simply refused. There was a lot of controversy surrounding Aileen's case. Especially the decision made to put her on death row. Psychologists, outside of the prison's command, believe that Aileen was not mentally fit to stand trial and therefore she should not have been able to make any demands as far as her sentencing. There were also a lot of biased opinions hanging over the trial from day one. Those biased opinions coming from the jury, the prosecution, as well as the judge. Many reporters and criminologists argue the fact that Wuornos did not have a fair trial, however, her execution date stood and she left this world the same way she had lived in it for so long. Alone.

Her life of crime started when she was young. Just like her father. She was a young girl, beautiful back in her golden years, and lived her life on the road. Whenever she needed money she would either prostitute, or steal, sometimes even rob at gunpoint to get what she wanted. She was also arrested a few times for assault, stealing ammo for her favorite gun and grand theft auto. That was the best she felt she could do in life. And for a young woman, that could be very damaging. Aileen seemed to love living a fast life filled with partying and crime. It was all she knew growing up so, to her, that was normal living. She figured everyone was doing the same. Until she had her first real run-in with the law.

One drunken night, a few months after her eighteenth birthday, Aileen was arrested for driving under the influence, disorderly conduct, and shooting a pistol out of the window while driving. She had hitchhiked all the way out to Jefferson County, Colorado, and had been living amongst different men, with whom she slept with for money and a place to lay her head. Aileen continued to trade on her looks to support herself, until her luck ran out in Colorado. She was hit with failing to appear in court for her three counts in Colorado, and ended up serving nearly two years in the county jail. After her release, Wuornos was in search of some place warm. She'd lost contact with previous clients and people who made sure she had a place to sleep at night and was right back on the streets where she began. Prostituting, rebuilding her brand, and sleeping in abandoned cars and rundown motels. She hated sleeping in the cold while living in the woods and abandoned cars in Michigan, and didn't want to do it in the snowy mountains of Colorado. As a child, her nights spent sleeping in the cold were terrible. There were times where she had no blankets or pillows. Just the clothes she was wearing on her back, and the limited shelter of an old car. Dawn stayed with her some nights, an added comfort to the little comfort she had, but that wasn't enough for Aileen. She needed stability. Especially at such a tender age in her life.

Colorado was better for her than back home in Troy, but it wasn't the life she wanted to live. She had access to more johns, more money, more opportunity. "Opportunity" being: meeting more men to sleep with for money. She often thought about where she would be if Keith had his own place and was able to take her in, but he was on the outs just like she was. He slept from pillow to post, wherever he could lay his head, with whatever friends around their hometown who would let him in. Although Keith had his own hardships in life he did his best to be there for his sister. Despite their upbringing and sibling rivalries they had gone through over the years, he loved his sister. He was one of the few people in her life whom she felt like loved her unconditionally. Their relationship had been tainted with their sexual interactions, so maybe that shielded Aileen's vision a bit, when it came to Keith. She looked to him as more of a companion than she did as her brother, some believe. And it's easy to comprehend why.

Once she left the snowy state of Colorado, Aileen headed to Florida. She stated to Dawn that she wanted to "sleep on the beach and enjoy the sun." Much understandable being that she had slept in the cold for years prior. However, her life of crime didn't stop when she finally reached her destination. She was arrested for assault and disturbing the peace after a nasty fight with her husband, at the time. She was arrested for drunk driving after her brother died. One night, after a fight with a

10

boyfriend that she really cared for, Wuornos got drunk out of her mind and held up a mini-mart. Wearing nothing but a bikini and waving her pistol, she robbed the mini-mart of $35 and two packs of cigarettes. For her crime, she was ordered to spend a full year in jail. Nothing new to an already spiraling Lee Wuornos. Just one year after her release, she was arrested in Key West, Florida for trying to cash several checks that were apparently stolen. And just a year later quickly became the key suspect in the robbery of an ammunition store in Pasco County, where a revolver and a box of ammunition was taken.

A year after that, Aileen made her way to the very south of Florida. Miami Beach. Where she was apprehended for the theft of a vehicle and resisting arrest and providing police with a fake ID. Her aunt's. In the car, Miami police found the stolen ammunition and the gun. A few months later, Aileen was detained by the Volusia County Sheriff's Department for questioning. She had been accused of pulling a gun on an ex-lover and robbing him of $200. Once patted down by authorities, she was found to be carrying stolen ammunition, and upon a vehicle search, was also found to be carrying the stolen gun underneath her passenger seat.

Chapter Two

Florida Living

By the time she was twenty years old, Aileen had finally decided to settle down in the springtime. Her place of choice, Daytona Beach, Florida. She took shelter in an old rundown motel called The Fairview Inn. It was her favorite place to stay, considering the many places she had slept previously. It wasn't long into her days of hooking on Florida's highways that she ran into a man she thought could be her saving grace. A man she thought would take away all of her money problems and set her up for life. She wasn't attracted to him really. He was just an old man who laid eyes on a pretty young thing and fell head-over-heels in love with her. To Aileen, he was a goldmine. She had been living her life on the road ever since she was a kid, and she was tired. She wanted out of the life she was living and wanted something to call her own. That was where Fell, fell into the picture. She even joked with her best friend back home, Dawn Botkins, about how much she only wanted Fell's money.

Lewis Gratz Fell was a retired Yacht Club President when he met Aileen Wuornos. As she stood on the side of the highway next to an abandoned car pretending to be a damsel in distress, he pulled over to be her knight in shining armor. For a man Lewis' age, 69 at the time, being with a twenty-year-old woman seemed like a dream come true. Contrary to her looks in her later years, Aileen was a very beautiful woman in 1976 and Gratz couldn't pass that up. After spending very little time getting to know each other, they quickly married and life as a married woman for Wuornos began. Fell was so happy to be married to a pretty young thing, he had their wedding published in the local newspapers' "society pages." In the world of wealth, Fell was a very popular man amongst his peers. He obtained a certain image in the eyes of the wealthy, and unbeknownst to him and his poor judgement of a pretty face, Aileen did not fit in with his crowd at all. She was impulsive. Explosive. Mean. Rude. Mannerless. Just all around ruthless, and Fell quickly regretted his decision to marry her.

Wuornos treated the old man terribly. She talked to him the way no man his age believed a woman should ever talk to a man. She continued her bar hopping, drinking, drugging and fighting. Her belligerent outbursts and going to jail also continued. You can imagine how much of a bad look that was for a former Yacht Club President. Fell was used to classy black-tie events. He was used to having a woman on his arm that he could take out in public, without having to worry about her being arrested by the end of the night because she had assaulted someone. Something Aileen Wuornos had been infamous for. When he finally caught on to the front that Aileen was putting on to get his money, he cut her off financially. That didn't go well for either of them. She flipped out and assaulted him. Pissed about the money she stopped receiving to go out drinking and partying, she wound up beating him with his own cane. Fell eventually filed a restraining order against her and quickly annulled their marriage, once again sending Aileen back to the same streets he had picked her up from.

Aileen was too set in her destructive ways to realize that she had actually found the way out she was looking for. As horrible as it sounds, settling down with Fell, even for just a short amount of time, had put her in a position to get some real help. Not only financially, but also mentally. Had she been adult enough to want better for herself in every which way, she could have used that marriage to seek the medical help she needed. However, no one was ever brave enough, or cared enough, to let her know that her mental health was more important than money. It was easy for Aileen to overlook her mental health. Her upbringing, and mental diagnosis, really damaged her mind and way of thinking. She thought about survival and that was it. Fell was too old of a man to take the time to get her help with that. He was also already retired. His retirement, to him, meant having a relaxing life for the rest of his days.

Lewis Fell wanted a good-looking woman on his arm, to have fun, good sex, and relax. Unfortunately, that was nowhere near, or far, with Aileen. She was still young, wild, and free. So, even though they had gotten married, she was still living her life as a single woman. On top of that, there was no real sexual attraction to him. He was merely another john she used to get what she wanted. And so did he. At least, that was the way she had looked at it. No man had ever paid her for anything other than sex and attention. Aileen didn't wholeheartedly believe that Lewis loved her the way he said he did. Because of her long list of men and the way they had always treated her, even throughout grade school, she didn't believe any man would ever love her. In her eyes, all they wanted was sex, and her husband was no different. Especially, given his age. He was seventy and she was twenty. It was all a contract in her eyes.

After Fell divorced Aileen, she decided to go back home to Michigan, catch up with her brother, and take in some much-needed family time. However, with the failed marriage hanging over her head, and the thoughts of her having to live her life on the road once again, she got drunk and lost her temper. While out at a bar on the night of July 14th, Wuornos was being her usual self. Drinking, smoking, and hanging around with all the guys and her temper got the best of her. Drunk and belligerent, upset at anyone who looked at her too hard, she snapped out and threw the cue ball from the pool table at the bartender's head. She was upset that he had cut her off from drinking. Police were

15

called and Aileen picked up another set of charges. Assault and disturbing the peace. She spent a few nights in jail after that. Nothing new to an already tainted rap-sheet. Then, on July 16th of 1976, just after being released from jail, a blow landed on Wuornos that hit her like a truck. She found out that Keith had died from throat cancer.

Keith was born in March of 1955. He was Diane and Leo's first child, older than Aileen by just about a year. He and Aileen had always been close. She was his little sister and did what he had to do in order to protect her. Though Keith had his own life and did his own thing, and he and his sister would fight like every other pair of siblings, he always made a way to check on her. Keith was the closest thing that Aileen had ever come to true unconditional love, in a weird way. To an outsider looking in, they would seem like the regular brother/sister duo, however, behind closed doors there was something far more sinister going on. To the two of them, their lives were normal, up until it came to the way their grandfather treated them. But, to people who were in their right minds, Keith and Aileen's relationship was very inappropriate. At times they looked like they were the happiest people in the world when they were with each other. And other times they fought like cats and dogs. Or, a couple who had just found out one or the other was cheating. Aileen was a tough little chick growing up. She had to be, considering where and how she had grown up, and Keith made sure he kept her on her toes. They even fistfought like two guys at times. It has been questioned whether or not Keith had a jealous streak in him when it came to Aileen, or was he just a concerned brother wanting to look after his little sister?

The pair had a very important bond. They were abandoned together, and even abused together. So, they had to look out for one another. To Keith, he and Aileen could fight all day if they wanted to, but if anyone else said or did something out of the way to her, he would take care of it. By the time Aileen was ten years old, she and Keith took their relationship to the next level. Literally. They started performing sexual acts on each other as a bonding mechanism. To them that was normal. They loved each other and that was just another way for them to show it. There has always been some doubt surrounding Aileen's allegations in a letter she wrote from prison about her and Keith, but those doubts were eventually put to rest when a friend of the family came forth and explained what he had seen with his own eyes.

Aileen actually enjoyed her sexual encounters with her brother, Keith. In fact, it happened on several occasions and she didn't make him trade anything for it, the way she would the rest of the neighborhood boys. Depending on the perspective in which you look at their lives, you might say what they were doing was innocent. It was not. They were young children, yes, but they knew what they were doing all along. They would even run away with each other at times, to escape their grandfather and continue their sexcapades. Eventually they were found and brought back home, but that didn't stop them from living their double lives. So, not only was Aileen attached to Keith as her big brother, she was attached to him physically. Sexually. When he died it was very hard for her. She'd experienced her first real loss of love and felt even more alone in the world. The last thing she received from Keith was ten thousand dollars from his life insurance policy, which she spent paying a $100 court fine and eventually blew the rest within two months. Aileen's life spiraled even more out of control after losing her brother. She blew the life insurance money on buying booze, drugs, hotel rooms, and a luxury car that she ended up wrecking not long after. And once again, landed herself some time behind bars for recklessly drinking and driving.

It isn't too unbelievable to say that Aileen's hungry hunt for love started after Keith had died. She lost her brother. Her friend. Her companion. But, most importantly, she lost a guy who loved her. In her eyes Keith was different from the other boys, he respected her body and treated her like a woman. Which was easier for him to do than the others, because she was his sister. In other words, Keith didn't treat her like a prostitute the way every other boy from the neighborhood had. To Aileen, that was something to be proud of. When she got older she wanted a guy like Keith. She wanted to be loved and helped, and taken care of, the way Keith had taken care of her in their younger years. Unfortunately, Aileen didn't pack the delicacy that other men craved. To them, she was nothing more than a quick rendezvous and a good time.

With a failed marriage, the loss of her brother, and empty pockets under her belt, Aileen hit the road again and headed back to Florida. She was back prostituting, sleeping from pillow to post and getting drunk in her favorite bars every night. With no real direction or goals set in her life, Aileen worked the highways all the way from north Florida, straight on down to as far south as she could get. She worked the exit ramps. Every truck stop. Even the rest stops along the highway. Nothing was beneath her because she felt like that was the best she could do anyway. At one point in time she met a guy she really liked. A guy who semi-reminded her of Keith. He took her in and let her stay with him, got her drunk, and hung out with her at their local bars. The Last Resort was one of their favorite joints to rock out at most nights.

She tried to commit suicide not long before she met him. She had already lost Keith, and not long after returning to Florida she got a call about her grandfather. The old man had committed suicide right there in his own garage. Though Aileen had never had a healthy relationship with the man she called her dad, who was actually her grandfather, hearing about his death struck a nerve for her. It brought back all of those cutting feelings and memories about her brother Keith, and she wanted to be the next to go. So, she got drunk and went down to the beach with her old trusty .22 and shot herself in the stomach. The shot caused some internal damage, but it didn't kill her. Florida doctors didn't seem to care much for her either, which didn't soften the blow at all for Aileen. She even told one of the nurses that it wasn't her first time trying to kill herself, in hopes of a little compassion. But, there was none. Usually, when a person comes into the ER after a bout of trying to commit suicide, they're admitted for mental evaluations. Sometimes even held against their will, however, Aileen was patched up and sent right back out the doors she had come through.

With her luck, she ran into a guy she thought could save her from herself. He managed for a while, but it didn't take long for the old Aileen Wuornos to appear and show him her true nature. The argument was believed to be about her being a working girl. She was always drunk and looking for her next trick, and most guys who are wanting to be in a committed relationship aren't fond of their woman turning tricks. To Aileen it was just a job. She didn't see the issue he had there and he ended up breaking things off with her. For a woman already suffering with abandonment issues, that wasn't something she could easily overlook. That same night, she got drunk and held up the mini-mart. It was merely a cry for his attention. She wanted to see if he would come to her aid the same way he had after she tried to kill herself. He did not. And once again, Aileen was on her own and down on her luck.

She didn't get too far away from the mini-mart before she was arrested. The old beat-up car she was driving during her stickup gave up on her just like everyone else in her life. The old piece of junk wound up overheating during her flee, forcing her to pull over on the side of the highway, where police spotted her and realized she fit the description. She was already no stranger to police in the area and they wasted no time hauling her in to face her punishment. Three years in a Florida state prison for armed robbery and a weapons charge. The longest bid Aileen had yet to serve. She spent her time in lockup reading her Bible and reflecting on all the wrong she'd done in her life. She thought about her longtime best friend, Dawn Botkins, one of the nicest people she'd ever met, according to her letters and interviews with Dawn. She also dreamed of getting out and getting back together with her boyfriend. The only thing she hadn't thought about was her mental health, getting her life together, and kicking her old habits.

As soon as she was released from the prison gates, she jumped right back into hitchhiking and prostitution. It was like she was born to live that life and had no intentions of ever giving it up. Realizing she'd lost contact with the boyfriend she so desperately longed for while on the streets, and in prison, she gave up on men entirely. She felt like any relationship she got into moving forward would fail, just like the rest of them, so there was no need for her to bother. Yet and still, she was still longing for some type of connection. She wanted to feel love from anywhere she could and it was slowly driving her insane.

By age 27, Aileen had made a vow to herself. One that she felt was long overdue. She was done giving any of her emotions to men. She still did her hitchhiking and prostituting in order to take care of herself, but when it came to any emotional connection, she was done. She hated men. Her extreme wants for a connection eventually took her over the fence, and she tried her hand with dating women. While she was incarcerated she saw lesbian activity and frowned upon it, but once on the outside and her patience with men had run out, she found the acceptance she was looking for from a woman she had met while getting drunk at The Last Resort. Twenty-four-year-old Tyria Moore.

Chapter Three

The Lesbians

By 1986 Aileen was more bitter than ever before. She was drunk, angry, and also lonely. When she ran into Tyria Moore at a gay bar in Daytona, she decided to test her hand. There was an instant attraction between the two, even though Wuornos' looks were deteriorating because of her savage lifestyle, Moore was still interested. That alone gave Aileen a feeling of acceptance she didn't think she had ever felt before. "Something only a woman can give you," she described in her letters. After hours of drinking and friendly conversation, Aileen felt inclined to leave the bar that night and go home with Tyria. The pair hit it off very well. Aileen felt like she had found her brother Keith, just a different version. She thought, maybe she should have been dating women all along. But then again, she was heavily into the Bible and felt like a relationship with a woman was not one that God would accept. However, that didn't stop her from having her companionship with Tyria.

Aileen and Tyria spent that entire weekend together. It was like a high school love for the both of them. They stayed locked away in Tyria's bedroom, only sneaking out to get food or use the bathroom, spending some much-needed quality time for the both of them. It had always been assumed that they spent their entire weekend having sex like a regular couple; Aileen says otherwise. Of course, they've had sexual encounters before, but it wasn't always pleasurable for either of them. In fact, Tyria often complained to a friend that they didn't have enough sex.

Although Aileen had made up her mind to give up on men, she was still very much attracted to them. She preferred sex with men over her sex with Tyria, but she loved Tyria. Their relationship was a strange one. It was like, Aileen wanted to be in a relationship with her, but she didn't. She craved the emotional connection more than she did the physical one, and Tyria didn't understand that right away. In her mind, she had found a woman who accepted her for who she was and wanted the experience to grow into a deep, meaningful relationship. With sex included. "Lee," a nickname given to Aileen by the bikers at her favorite biker bar, had never been into women a day in her life, but she had that connection with Tyria and almost immediately, they became inseparable.

Everything was great for them in the beginning. They quickly moved in together, staying in a room at the Fairview Inn. Sometimes couch surfing at a friend's place. There were even points in their relationship where they slept in the woods together because they could no longer afford their rent. The couple became notorious around Daytona Beach, strictly because of their lifestyle. Being gay back then, especially in the south, was one of the most distasteful sins a person could ever commit. But, Tyria, nor Lee, cared what anyone thought. Lee even got into bar fights to protect what she felt was rightfully hers. And that was Tyria.

At first, Tyria had no idea how Lee made her money. All she knew was that she was being taken care of. She got all the booze she wanted. All the drugs she could handle. She got to go out to the bars every night and have a good time, and most importantly, she had a place to rest her head most of the time. She was enjoying her life in Florida more than she did back home in Pennsylvania, and it was all thanks to Lee. When she did find out that Lee was a hitch-hiking hooker, she strongly disapproved. It didn't matter much to Aileen that her lover didn't want her going around town sleeping with every man she could get her hands on, that was how she ensured they had a place to stay and food in their stomachs. So, Tyria would have to deal with it, all the while continuing to keep their relationship going.

Like always, Aileen's temper had been lingering at the surface. One afternoon, Tyria decided she would try once more to get her lover to stop selling her body to men. She was more than willing to go back to work and get them on their feet the right way and felt like it wasn't too much to ask of Lee. However, Aileen wasn't having it. She was used to fast money, fast living, and doing whatever it was that she wanted to do. That afternoon was the first time Tyria met the lady of rage that Aileen had been trying so hard to keep contained. She flew off the handle while they were out drinking at their favorite bar. For a woman like Tyria, being talked to like the scum of the earth, in public, was embarrassing. She was also able to quickly point out that Aileen had other issues she refused to deal with. Mental issues. There were instances where they would go grocery shopping and Aileen would have an angry outburst if someone looked at them wrong. In her eyes, people were judging their lesbian lifestyle and that wasn't ok with her. She didn't have the ability to know that there were things a lot of people disapproved of and sometimes she should turn the other cheek.

Tyria never expressed that to her again because she didn't want to be caught in the line of fire with Aileen. Nonetheless, she stayed by her lover's side. She really cared for Aileen and masked the many outbursts with excuses such as the stress of not having money and their living situation. She continued to follow Aileen wherever she went. Tyria could have easily dumped Aileen and went back home to live with her sister, but she truly cared for her. She saw something deep down inside that drew her in. At times, she even felt sorry for Aileen because she was mentally incapable of doing anything other than what she was already doing. And that was living her life on the road.

As their relationship grew older, Aileen grew even more fond of Tyria. Although she never considered herself to be a lesbian, she went around town referring to Tyria as her "wife." Everyone in Daytona Beach knew who they were and what they meant to each other. Much like Keith, Tyria was a voice of reason for Aileen. Not much reasoning got done by either of them, but in a way they did keep her somewhat grounded. Had it not been for Tyria coming into Aileen's life when she had, Wuornos might have started her killing spree much earlier.

The fun with Tyria was a break for Aileen, almost a distraction from what was next to come. They bar hopped. Hitchhiked. Spent sunny days at the beach. Watched their favorite TV shows. Anything a normal couple would do, the two of them did together. Tyria was much like Dawn for Aileen. A real friend whom she could talk to without much judgement. The only real human interaction Aileen had ever had was with men. Even at a young age in her life, so when she met Tyria and got that feeling of completion she had been longing for, she clung to it for dear life. She was so grateful to have Tyria in her world, she would actually spend weekends working the highway to gather up enough money to have month-long hotel stays. She paid for everything Tyria wanted, and had even funded a trip for Tyria's sister to visit Florida from Pennsylvania.

In times of pity, Tyria knew she was all Aileen had in the world. She knew about Dawn, back home in Michigan, but in their current times,

Aileen was a lost soul with no one to care for her or comfort her. It broke Tyria's heart behind closed doors because she knew that a life with Aileen was not what she wanted forever. Mostly due to the way Aileen behaved and carried herself. She was an embarrassment and she didn't even recognize it in herself. She was unteachable, unsavable, and most certainly unmanageable. For a normal person, like Tyria, that was a recipe for disaster. She wanted more for herself in life and knew that would be impossible to have with Aileen on her arm.

There were times where Aileen would get so jealous about Tyria's interactions with anyone other than her, that she would lash out and throw things, or curse the person out just to get them away from Tyria. Aileen saw no issues with that, in fact, she often laughed it off and disguised it as a joke. Tyria knew better, and she started to resent their relationship. Yet and still, she continued hanging on in hopes that something would change.

By then, Aileen had been working the Florida highways for more than a decade. Not a road she wasn't already used to traveling. Her lifestyle had really started to show on her once gorgeous figure and face, and her days as the much-desired damsel in distress quickly started to come to its closing. She was thirty-three years old by the spring of 1989 and looked much older. She also dressed more ruggish, wearing her jeans and baseball caps. Her figure looked more like a truck driver to men, than it did a hooker. However, some of them still paid to have a good time with her. Tyria had grown accustomed to Aileen bringing home hundreds of dollars a day in the beginning, to then only being able to bring home what some would refer to as "scraps."

Eventually, Aileen caught on to Tyria's frustration. She feared that her lover was going to leave her high and dry and go back home to her family in Pennsylvania. Already knowing what it was like to lose the closest person to her, she became desperate. She was willing to do just about anything to keep Tyria happy and comfortable. Her days in the world of prostitution were very limited and she feared committing another robbery that would get her locked away from Tyria, so she had to do something. And fast. She was able to scrape up enough cash for them to hit the road together, and that's what they did. Gathered up what little belongings they had and hit the road to Homosassa Springs, Florida. The goal when they got there was to start all over and resurface bigger and better. Tyria got herself another job, working at the hotel they were staying at, and "Lee" continued her hitch-hiking hooker routine. She figured it was a new city, there would be new men, men who didn't know her, and she would start making the money she was used to making again. The plan seemed like a gem to Aileen, whereas Tyria, was more focused on legal work. She was tired of Aileen giving herself to men. She didn't want to share Aileen with the sleazebags she had to. Even more, she knew the dangers of being a sex-worker and she didn't want anything to happen to the woman she cared about.

Unfortunately, the men in the Springs weren't too fond of her either. It came to a point where Tyria grew tired of Lee always being on the road, but returning with little to no money. The burden of making sure they had a roof over their head and food in their bellies was solely on her at that point and she couldn't take it. What was good for the goose, turned out not to be good for the gander. However, Aileen was so afraid of Tyria leaving her alone, she grew even more desperate. She started staying on the road even longer, doing whatever she could to gain the interest of more men. Then, came the turning point that there was no turning back from. She ran into fifty-one-year-old Richard Mallory, on the highway just outside of Tampa, Florida.

Mallory was an electronics repairman who owned his own shop in Clearwater, Florida. Unbeknownst to a lot of the public during Aileen's trial, Mallory had a bit of a violent criminal history. He served ten years in a state prison for rape. Mallory was known for his craze with getting drunk, meeting different women, and being highly paranoid. A habit more than likely formed while serving time in the state pen. The man didn't even keep regular employees working at his shop for too long. The only time he ever hired any extra help was when he'd come home from a trip and needed help putting his orders away. Taking trips away from home for days at a time wasn't something outside of his norm, so when he didn't call anyone or show up for work for a few days, no one really suspected anything. It wasn't until police found his Cadillac abandoned off the side of the highway that anyone got suspicious.

Lee's pickup routine was to stand on the highway next to any old abandoned car, and wait for a man to see her and ask if she needed some help. Mallory was on his way out of town to Daytona when he ran into Lee. He wasn't too friendly right off the bat. Claiming that she was lucky

29

he even stopped to see if she needed help, and complained that with her looks, she would be lucky if any man even looked twice at her. Right away, that set Aileen off. She was used to being talked to like she meant nothing, but after she'd made the vow to herself to be done with men, she refused to take any more of their verbal abuse. She and Mallory bickered with each other for a while before they agreed on a price for the sex. He was supposed to pay her a whopping ten dollars up front, and the rest when they were finished. However, it was all just a game to Mallory, according to Aileen. He wanted to tie her up and have anal sex. Something she wasn't too trustworthy of. Something about him just didn't sit right with her, so she refused the sex and tried to get out of the car to pick up her next john.

That was when he got rough and rowdy with her. She claims he grabbed her, smacked her around a bit, and tried to rape her. She fought him off as best she could and eventually pulled out her gun and shot him four times. Twice in the chest and twice in the back. A killing that Aileen claims was self-defense. There was a bit of a panic after she'd shot and killed Mallory, but not soon after, with him still dead in the driver's seat, Aileen rummaged through his pockets and robbed him of the money he owed her. She even took what little valuables he had in his car with him. After that, she wrapped his body up in an old carpet runner she found lying in the woods, drug him a little ways away from the crime scene and took off in his Cadillac.

The first thing she did when she got back to the hotel that night, was tell Tyria about what she had done. Her lover didn't believe her at first, because of the way she told the story. It was almost as if she were bragging about taking a man's life. It seemed too fanciful for Tyria to believe, but she did have her doubts. She'd seen how outrageous Aileen could get at times. She even flipped out on Tyria's sister while she visited, telling her if she was going to be there with them any longer she needed to get herself a job. She only said that because she wanted Tyria all to herself. It wasn't until Aileen pulled out a wad of money she'd gotten off Mallory and his stolen valuables that Tyria actually believed that she had really killed a man. The women quickly packed up their belongings that same night, abandoned their hotel room and hit the road in search of a new place to call home. For the time being. Tyria never went to the police about what she knew because she was afraid of Aileen. Murder was a huge step away from her usual outburst and bar fights. She didn't want to end up next on Aileen's laundry list of victims.

Richard Mallory's body was found two weeks after police discovered his abandoned Cadillac. Two kids searching the woods for scrap metal came across his decaying corpse and notified the Volusia County police. His body had been so badly decomposed under the Florida sun, his hands had to be cut off and taken into forensics in order to get a proper ID on him. In search of any leads, police spent months investigating Richard's lifestyle to see what they could come up with. There was nothing. Eventually, they came across a stripper that Mallory was a regular with. A woman by the name of Chastity. She had told her boyfriend one night while they were arguing that she was the one who had killed Richard Mallory, a story that would soon nearly cost her

31

freedom. It was proven that her story was all a fabricated lie because she was mad at her boyfriend. The real killer, Aileen Wuornos, had covered her tracks well for the time being. Police were under the impression that they were dealing with a man who knew what he was doing, when in fact, it was a woman all along. What duped them was the body being drug away from the crime scene. Mallory was a big guy, so it was hard for authorities to believe that a woman was able to move him that far away from the crime scene and not leave a shred of evidence. Eventually, Mallory's case went cold and police had to rely on time before they could bring down their killer.

Chapter Four

Damsel of Death

After her first murder, Aileen's lover felt like she had gotten all of her frustrations out and she would finally be done with her life of crime. But, that was a hard reach for Tyria, and also Wuornos. She fell in love with the thrill after killing Richard Mallory. Figuring since she hadn't seen anything on the news, or been contacted by the police about the murder, she was in the clear. What Aileen didn't know was that it was only a matter of time before her trail of bodies would find their ways back to her. She held on to her sanity for about six months before deciding to strike again. Her M.O.: Robbery. She wanted money. Her looks had given out on her for good by that time and since Tyria didn't want her prostituting anymore anyway, Wuornos made that her reason to kill. If she was going to continue taking care of them she needed the funds to do so, and that was how she did it.

Police were highly thrown off after finding bodies back to back in different counties across South West, Florida. At one point they weren't even sure if they were dealing with the same killer for each victim. Two killers, or multiple copy-cat killers. What gave Aileen the leverage she had, was that she was unique in her style. Police weren't thinking of getting their hands on a female serial killer. They were used to hauling in men who killed in the same manner that Aileen had. If her weapon of choice had been poison, or her victims had been people she actually knew, she may have been brought to justice a lot sooner than she had.

David Spears, a forty-three-year-old construction worker out of Sarasota, Florida, was found dead. Naked and shot six times in the upper body. His remains were found about forty miles north of Tampa in Citrus County. He was a heavy equipment operator who was last seen by his boss weeks before his body was found. David informed his boss that he would be heading to Orlando for work, but he never made it. When his boss went to the authorities about it, they started an investigation and later found his truck abandoned off interstate 75. The doors were unlocked and the license plate had been removed. A tactic Wuornos used to deter police from finding out who owned the vehicle right away. Detectives also noted that there was a used condom found near the body. Something they hadn't seen at any other crime scenes.

Over in Pasco County, thirty miles south of where Richard Mallory's body was found, another decaying body was found off interstate 75 on June 6th. The body had been sitting for so long in the hot Florida sun, medical examiners weren't able to get any fingerprints from their victim, nor were they able to estimate a time of death for the guy. The nine bullets they pulled out of the corpse were decaying right along with the body, but detectives were quickly able to pinpoint that they were from a .22 caliber pistol and figured they must have been dealing with the same killer in the previous murder. Their John Doe was later identified as forty-year-old Charles "Chuck" Carskadon. He was a part-time rodeo worker whom Aileen also claimed to have murdered in self-defense. She said that after she shot him once he said, "you bitch, I'm going to die." And her response to that was, "I guess you are. You were gonna kill me anyway."

Peter Siems was on his way from Florida to New Jersey when he came across Wuornos. She was standing on the side of the highway near an old abandoned car, like she would any other time she picked up a john, and he pulled over to see if she needed any help. The people in his life described the sixty-five-year-old man as being highly religious, very easygoing, and just an all-around gentleman. No one could testify that he had ever had a violent streak towards any of the women in his life, therefore they didn't believe Aileen's claim of self-defense. The number of times he was shot has never been determined, because Peter Siems' body has never been found. His abandoned car had later been found in Orange Springs on July 4, 1990. Two witnesses testified in court that they had seen both Aileen, and Tyria Moore, driving Siems' car. Detectives had strong evidence linking Aileen to the stolen vehicle as well. In the end, detectives pressured Wuornos on Peter Siems' whereabouts, but she denied having any interactions with him at all, and with nothing else to go on they lost all hopes of finding him alive, or dead.

Fifty-year-old Eugene Troy Burress was a sausage salesman that had been reported missing on July 31st. He was also described as a very respectable man amongst his community. His abandoned delivery truck was found in a forest in Ocala, Florida, and his decaying body was found four days later by a pair of campers. Wuornos stated during interviews with police that he laughed at her before he tried to rape and kill her, leading her to shoot him twice in the chest out of self-defense. When asked why she hadn't gone to the police sooner, she said, "who would believe a hitch-hiking hooker?" She wasn't totally wrong in her thinking in that instance. There are numerous reports of female sex-workers whose rapes are overlooked just because of their line of work. However, that's no excuse for Aileen's behavior. She killed out of greed and selfishness.

Psychological studies have shown that Aileen suffered from borderline personality disorder, as well as anti-social disorder and her killings were merely stemmed from her childhood. She ran into older men who were scum, much like her grandfather, and it brought back all those painful memories from her past, so she shot and killed them. Some experts say she was killing her grandfather over and over again. Also, the boys from her school that she would sleep with for loose change and cigarettes. She had suffered a lot of abuse at the hands of so many different men, especially the johns she picked up on the road. At that point in her life she was done tolerating men in general. So, she shot and killed them, and also robbed them of their belongings. Much like the way she was robbed of her innocence as a child. To her it all made sense. She was getting her payback from a life that had dealt her a crappy hand.

Aileen had shot and killed four men over the course of a few months. She'd gotten so comfortable with having a steady stream of income and being able to pay the bills on time, that she didn't stop for one second to think about the "what if's." By then, Tyria claimed to be even more afraid of her, so she wouldn't dare go to the police and tell what she knew, and Aileen just kept right on killing and robbing. Not only that, but Wuornos has gone on the record to say that Tyria was the one who actually pressured her to make more and more money. She didn't care how she made it, as long as she made it. She was enjoying reaping the benefits from the lifestyle Aileen lived. While the money was pouring in she was perfectly fine. But, when the money started to run low again, she would threaten to leave Aileen and go back home to Pennsylvania. To a person with an upbringing like Wuornos, that played a huge role in the way her brain processed her crimes. She felt like she had to kill those men in order to keep her one true love by her side. If she didn't, Tyria would leave her like her mother and father. Her husband. And her brother Keith.

On July 4th, Aileen allowed Tyria to drive Peter Siems' car while she sat in the passenger seat and got drunk. They were headed nowhere in particular, just out enjoying a ride before settling down to watch fireworks. Tyria took a curve going too fast and flipped their vehicle. Aside from a nasty cut on Aileen's arm, neither of the women were hurt too badly. Dazed and shaken, they escape from the turned-over car and try to gather their composure. Tyria wanted to wait for the police and ambulance, just in case they were seriously injured, but Aileen had other plans. The car they were in belonged to a dead Peter Siems and she didn't want any involvement with the police, in fear of being questioned about his murder.

A few of her johns told police that she carried a "kill bag." Inside, she kept a bottle of Windex and hand towels to wipe away her fingerprints. A change of underwear. Condoms, and her old trusty .22. The day of the accident was the first time Tyria learned of the kill bag. Aileen quickly ripped the license plate off the back of the vehicle, with her bare hands, and threw it far into the woods. She then started to spray the inside of the car with Windex and wipe away their prints. She also wiped away their prints from the outside of the car as well. Confused, Tyria questioned why her lover felt the need to wipe away their fingerprints. She had a gut feeling that Aileen had stolen the car from another victim, just like she did the first time. However, Aileen told her the only issue they had was that she had rented the car with a phony ID. Tyria didn't believe that, but didn't question her any further because she was afraid that she would end up next on the kill list.

Ronda Bailey, a witness for the prosecution, called the accident in to the police. She was sitting on her front porch at the time and saw the whole thing. It was weird to her that the women were in such a hurry to get away from the scene of the accident, she even asked them if they wanted to come inside and use her phone. She said that Tyria didn't say too much of anything. It was "Lee" who had done all the talking, and screaming, and cursing. Aileen gave her a phony story about her father living just up the road and they were on their way to visit him. Needless to say, Ronda didn't believe them and pointed out the direction in which they were headed to the paramedics who arrived at the scene before the police.

As they trotted up the road away from the accident, paramedics pulled alongside them and asked if they were the two women who had just been involved in an accident. Tyria kept her mouth shut and let Lee do all the talking. Being her usual smart-mouthed self, Wuornos told the two men they weren't involved in any accidents, they didn't need any help, they were just trying to hitch a ride back to Daytona. The paramedics didn't believe her, but let them continue on their way.

Police found Peter Siems' car abandoned in Marion County. They used the vin number in order to find the registered owner, because Aileen had discarded the license plate, but no Peter Siems. Siems' wife had already reported him missing, so when police found his abandoned car and the eyewitness to the crash, they sent out a nationwide alert,

39

along with a sketch of the two women seen leaving the scene of the car accident. Aileen Wuornos and Tyria Moore. Calls began to pour in almost immediately. A lot of people were very familiar with "Lee" and "Ty," nicknames they used in different areas. And it was long before police figured out who the real "Lee" was. When Siems' body was found, eventually, it was so badly decomposed that his wife had to identify him by his wedding ring.

Marion County Lead Investigator John Tilley was down on his luck with leads in Troy Burress' case. Because of Aileen's slick and sneaky murder style, he felt like he would never be able to crack the case and give Troy's family any closure. It wasn't until the sketches of Lee and Ty were released that a new light bulb went off in his head. When he learned that both Citrus and Pasco Counties had also found dead decaying bodies in the woods, all shot by the same caliber of pistol as his victim, he decided to take a trip to meet up with them. Once he met up with Lead Detective Jerry Thompson, who was handling the case of David Spears, and Lead Detective Tom Muck, who was handling the case of Charles Carskadon, the connections in their cases were very obvious.

However, what little information they had about the murders didn't stop Aileen from picking up and slaying victims. Fifty-year-old Charles "Dick" Humphreys fell next on her list of dead johns. He was a retired police officer and had also retired from his position as an Air Force Major earlier on. Wuornos shot him six times in his upper body. About one month later, another body was discovered. Walter Gino Antonio. The sixty-year-old's body was found off a logging road in Dixie County,

Florida. He was shot four times in the torso and left for dead wearing nothing but his tube socks. Antonio was a member of the reserve police in his earlier years. Towards the end of his life he worked as a truck driver and even did security part-time in between. His abandoned car was found just five days after his naked body was discovered in the woods.

When the investigation heated up detectives centered their hunt around Ocala, the largest city in Marion County. Munster, a special agent who worked for the FBI, was brought on board to work the homicides. His strong history in the sexual assaults of minors was what landed him the gig. In Munster's expertise, he believed the fact that each victim had been shot primarily in the torso meant something very important for the case. In his eyes, male killers were point-blank with it. They went for headshots more than anything. Whereas female killers aimed for the lower parts of the body. The torso was an easy target for inexperienced female shooters.

It was Munster's idea to get the sketches out to the public. Not only did he want to warn civilians of the dangers of picking up hitchhikers, but wanted to throw a twist in the killer's plans. No one stopped to pick up hitchhikers anymore and the killings quickly died down. Once their sketches started to circulate all across the state of Florida, Tyria grew nervous and decided to flee the state. She told Wuornos that she was going home to visit her sister for Thanksgiving, but that she would be back. In fact, Tyria didn't want to be implicated in the murders and had no plans on returning home to Wuornos. Or going to the police. She returned a little after Thanksgiving to return the ring Wuornos had given her and to pick up the rest of her things, so that she could move on with her life. She didn't disclose to her lover that the reason she was leaving was because she had seen their sketches on the news. It wasn't until she and Lee got into a fight about her leaving that she told her the sketches looked too much like them. Wuornos did her best to make Ty stay, but her lover was too afraid of being caught up.

The breakup was crucial for an already abandoned Aileen. Feeling helpless and weak, she started drinking more and more just to feel numb throughout the day. Especially, during sex with her johns. The more her heart broke, the more she isolated herself. She was so heartbroken after Tyria left her that she couldn't stand selling her body anymore. All she could do was drink and sleep. Eventually, she ended up having to pawn her lover's ring just to buy food and booze. When that $20 ran out, Aileen found herself broke, heartbroken and homeless once again, and had no choice but to sleep on an abandoned car seat in the back of her favorite bar "The Last Resort."

It was the thumbprint on a pawn shop receipt that gave detectives their big break. Aileen had pawned the majority of the valuables she pick-pocketed from her dead victims. Had it not been for pawn shop owners requiring a fingerprint, as well as ID, before handing over cash for valuables, police may have never caught on to who their killer was. After running the thumbprint through the police database, they discovered that the ID used to pawn the items and the identity of the thumbprint did not match up. They were looking for a woman by the name of Aileen Lee Wuornos. It didn't take long to track her down either. Two undercover detectives, by the name of Bucket and Drums, followed her every move for about two days before they finally made the decision to bring her into custody. They disguised themselves as two drug dealers from Atlanta looking to have a good time. Lee felt comfortable enough to sit and chat with them over drinks. She didn't suspect anything at all because she kept herself so drunk to escape the pain of no longer having her "wife" by her side.

Bucket and Drums were almost detected when a pair of Marion County police officers brought Wuornos outside of the bar for questioning. If it weren't for Bucket and Drums being quick on their feet, the whole case would have fallen through and Aileen might have had a chance to flee, much like Tyria. The two detectives quickly called in to the Marion County's Sheriff's Office and told their commander to have his officers back off, and the next day they made their arrest.

Chapter Five

End of the Road

Tyria Moore was located in Pennsylvania when the hammer came down on Aileen. She had been hiding out at her sister's place, hoping the law wouldn't catch up to her. She loved Wuornos and never wanted to turn on her, but she did what she had to do to keep herself from going to prison. Snitching on Aileen was her get out of jail free card. Detectives informed Moore of her role in getting Wuornos to confess to the crimes. She knew that if she didn't get that confession, or at least get Wuornos talking about what she had done, she would sit right next to her in a jail cell. The first call to Moore came in a few days after she'd been set up in a hotel in Daytona. She was instructed to let Wuornos know that police had been contacting her family about her involvement in the murders. Aileen was confident that she was only in jail for one of her petty warrants, but Tyria knew otherwise. She didn't let Wuornos know right off the bat that she had been picked up for the murders because detectives wanted to pull a confession out of her, but when the gloves came off she got right down to business.

It took her days to get to that point, as Aileen kept talking in circles because she knew the phone calls were being recorded, however, once Moore finally laid down the law, Wuornos told her to do what she had to do. She made it clear to detectives that Moore had no involvement in any of the murders and that it was alright for her to tell them what she knew.

There were several eyewitnesses brought on the stand to testify during Wuornos' trial, and Tyria Moore was the main one. Moore had been contacted for book and movie deals, right alongside her lover, so it wasn't clear of whether or not the jury should believe a word out of her mouth. It's been speculated that Moore was a willing accomplice and she only switched her role in the story in order to avoid jail time. She was the only one who could paint a vivid picture of Wuornos' state of mind during the four years they had been together, and the prosecution relied on that heavily.

The lovers had only seen each other one time since Wuornos was arrested, and it seemed to be the last. Moore did her best to avoid any eye

45

contact at all with Wuornos in the courtroom. Either she was ashamed to be her co-defendant, or she still had love for Wuornos and hated herself for having to testify against her. They did, however, lock eyes one time during the entire trial. There were no nasty or wicked outbursts from Wuornos as Tyria took the stand, though Moore did shoot her ex-lover a weak and bearable smile.

The most damaging testimony came from Moore's own lips. The one murder that would have given Wuornos a little bit of leverage, Moore had a different story about. Richard Mallory. Unbeknownst to a lot of the public, Mallory had a criminal history himself. A violent one. He'd spent ten years in prison for rape. The night Aileen crossed his path, she said that he had gotten rough with her and tried to rape her, so she shot him in self-defense. Moore testified to the complete opposite. It is unclear if authorities planted that story in Moore's head, or if it was the truth. Aileen swears that her first murder was self-defense and Mallory's criminal history had been left out of court findings, so it isn't too unbelievable.

Eleven recorded phone conversations, between Moore and Wuornos, were allowed to be played during the trial. Beforehand, Wuornos believed she was speaking with her lover in complete privacy and said some things on her own that were severely damaging to her case. Once she realized that the calls were being recorded and what Ty had been asking of her, she gave up the fight entirely. "Don't worry. I'll take the rap," she told Tyria. The assistant public defender didn't believe for one second that Tyria wasn't involved. She may not have murdered anyone, but she knew what Aileen had been doing all along. However, Tyria never confessed to anything, other than discussing book and movie deals with detectives, and how she had lied to her lover in order to get her to confess. Moore wanted off the hook completely, and that was the deal she got in exchange for Wuornos' life.

During her taped confession with police, Wuornos made it a point to make two things very clear. 1. Moore had nothing to do with any of the murders. And 2. Nothing she had done was Moore's fault. It wasn't until later during her trial that she semi-changed her story. She was upset with Ty for betraying her the way that she had and ultimately voiced that it was Ty who had turned the heat up on her. She felt so pressured to keep bringing in the money that kept Moore happy and comfortable. As it's been stated before, when the money was being raked in, Moore had no real complaints. But, it was when the money started to run low that Moore wanted more. In more than one way, Tyria absolutely played a major role in Aileen's murders. For one, she knew about them, and two, she played on Aileen's abandonment and mental issues in order to get what she wanted. She knew that Wuornos was deeply attached to her and would do whatever she had to do in order to keep her around. Even murder.

Without victim testimony, the prosecution had to rely on the evidence left behind and Wuornos herself. There was substantial evidence left behind. The pawn shop tickets for the victim's stolen property, a bloody handprint, and detectives had even found a storage locker in her name containing other items from her victims. Wuornos' lawyers were so furious when the prosecution introduced evidence from the other murders that he demanded a mistrial. In a way he was right to make that call, however, evidence from other cases is allowed to be presented in the courtroom if it has ties to the case at hand. Stephen Siems, son of Peter Siems took the stand to identify some of his father's belongings that were found in Wuornos' storage bin. They were all personal items. His license plate, a shaving kit, suit jacket. His testimony helped paint the picture the prosecution wanted painted all along. They didn't want Wuornos to be seen as just a killer, they wanted the jury to see her as a serial killer.

Going against her lawyers' commands, Wuornos made it a point to get on the stand herself and tell the story the way she wanted it to be heard. From a point of view of self-defense. She and her team were up against a tough prosecution who already had a mountain of evidence against her, which made her lawyers feel like she would be able to control her emotions while she was on the stand. She'd had several nasty outbursts during her trial, even towards the judge, they didn't want her to rack up any more charges. Her attorneys never said why they had actually allowed her to take the stand, maybe they had just run out of options. Some believe it's because Wuornos actually wanted them to argue for the death penalty and her testimony would make it even easier for them to argue.

Trisha Jenkins, assistant public defender, did her best to let Wuornos describe a scene where she was in fact the victim. Although that didn't turn over too smoothly for her defense, she had no other choice but to let Wuornos speak. It was either that, or Wuornos would fire her team and get a new one. It was evident that Wuornos made up her story as she spoke. Her tales were very different from the ones she first told the police when they brought her in. On the stand, she said that Mallory wanted more than just sex. She described him as a pain freak. She said that he had anally raped her while her hands were bound to the steering wheel of his car. She also added that he poured rubbing alcohol on her sexual organs to intensify her pain, and that he'd strangled her with a piece of electrical cord.

In the story she recapped on the stand, the only way she made it out alive was because she was so afraid to die at the hands of Richard Mallory. She described her struggle to untie her hands, go for her pistol and shoot him. She says that even though she had shot him, Mallory was still coming towards her. She shouted out a warning that she would shoot again, but the man kept coming towards her, leaving her with no choice but to riddle him with bullets. When asked why she would take the time to hide his body if she had shot him in self-defense, she said, "I didn't want the birds to peck at him."

Her reasoning for not giving detectives the gruesome details of the rape during her taped confession, was that she was incoherent. They picked her up from a bar where she had been drinking all night with little to no sleep. She says she doesn't remember what she said or didn't say. Which isn't completely unbelievable, considering she was going through a heartbreak and had been drinking all night. She also says that detectives kept cutting her off and wouldn't let her get her entire story out before they locked her up. They had their minds already made up about Aileen and her murders, all they needed to hear her say was that she did it. Not the how's or why's.

Her attorneys were carefully listening to the defense and made sure to instruct Wuornos not to answer certain questions, or reply to the sarcasm thrown at her by the defense with the intentions of making her upset. They knew that when someone said something Wuornos didn't agree with, she lashed out in extreme anger and spilled the truth. Tanner deliberately brought up facts from her other murder cases to purposely throw her off. He wanted the jury to see her as untrustworthy, murderous, and unremorseful. She proved him to be correct with a few of her outbursts. At one point she even had to be escorted out of the courtroom because she continued to make violent threats towards the judge and the jurors. When it came to her sentencing, the prosecution relied solely on Aileen's testimony. They were so confident that their case was solid, they felt no need to use the dozens of other testimonies from other witnesses to seal the deal. Wuornos would be sentenced to death, which is exactly what she wanted. She made her demands clear from the start. If she was found guilty, she didn't want to spend the rest of her life in prison, she wanted to be sentenced to death.

On January 27, 1992 the jury came to their conclusion in just 90 minutes. Guilty. Immediately, Wuornos jumped to her feet and cursed at all twelve of the jurors. Making idle threats and also stating that she hoped they, and their children, get raped in the ass. After the verdict, jurors have to listen to more evidence and testimony before deciding her fate. They sat through testimony from a fingerprint expert, corrections officers, and a private investigator. All of whom had concluded that Wuornos was nothing more than a cold-blooded killer. They also heard testimony from a psychologist, called by the defense, that they were not moved by. Aileen's own outburst had sealed her fate with the jury.

Wuornos seemed to be pleasantly pleased with her sentence. It's what she wanted from the very beginning. Her lawyers pleaded with her to continue going to her appeals, but she completely refused. She didn't want to sit through the agony of hearing any more people belittle her, bring up her mess of a life. She was ready to get it over with. She's gone on record repeatedly stating that. "I'm just ready to get it over with." Wuornos also made it very clear that if she wasn't put to death she would definitely kill again.

There were no trials for the murders of Dick Humphreys, Troy Burress, or David Spears. Wuornos simply pleaded no contest and took whatever the judge handed to her. She said she wanted to get right with God, and going back to trial for those murders would only deter her from her path. She ultimately confessed that Mallory was the only man whom she had actually killed in self-defense. The others were strictly for the thrill and the money. She did plead guilty to the murder of Charles Carskadon, earning herself her fifth death sentence. When she finally confessed to the murder of Gino Antonio, she was given her death date. No charges were ever brought against her for Peter Siems, because his body was never found. For a while there was talk about her receiving a new trial for the murder of Richard Mallory, not that it would bring forth a different outcome, but there was none. The supreme court had acknowledged all sixth death penalties. In an appeal letter written to the supreme court, she stated, "I am one who seriously has to be put down. Because I will kill again." It was after that letter that Governor Jeb Bush signed off on her death warrant. He ordered for her to be mentally evaluated beforehand, and all findings showed that Wuornos knew and understood the nature of her crimes. She also understood the severity of her sentence and was "ready to get it over with." She was executed by lethal injection at 9:47 A.M. on October 9, 2002.

The last words Aileen Lee Wuornos spoke were, *"I'd just like to say that I'm sailing with the rock and I'll be back. Like Independence day with Jesus. June 6th, like the movie. Big mothership and all, I'll be back."* The Rock is in reference to God. While in prison, she got closer to God. She'd always kept him in the back of her mind, but it wasn't until she'd been locked away to face the punishments for her crimes that she'd gotten closer. For years she claimed that her actions were purely out of self-defense, but after getting right with her Lord and Savior she came clean and confessed to killing all seven men.

Before her death, Wuornos was being propositioned with book and movie deals left and right. It's suspected that she fabricated her story so much during her trial because she was under the impression that it would make for a good movie. She wanted the profits to be able to take care of herself while she awaited her death. Unfortunately, Florida passed a law that prohibited felons to see any profit from crimes as horrendous as the ones Wuornos committed.

Wuornos was indeed a non-remorseful, cold-blooded murderer. It's easy for like-minded empaths to be sympathetic towards her life's story, however, her crimes are completely intolerable. She said herself that she was a person who needed to be put down. She made it very clear that if she wasn't, she would kill again. She also made it very clear that she hated people. The prosecution saw her to be a man-hating lesbian, but it was people in general that Aileen hated. She was very anti-social, though she kept in contact with her longtime best friend, Dawn Botkins, and her lover Tyria Moore. Those seemed to be the only two people she could tolerate throughout her life. Here are a few of her most infamous quotes to back up her testimony:

"I am a serial killer. I would kill again." Aileen was sure to let the court know, as well as every juror sitting on the stand, that she would do it again if given the chance to. To her, it was a scare tactic. One that would ensure she got the death penalty she was looking for, so that she wouldn't have to rot in her prison cell. "I need to die for the killings of those people. I robbed them and I killed them as cold as ice, and I would do it again. And I know I would kill another person because I've hated humans for a long time." She confessed during a recorded interview just days before she was set to take her last breath. "I wanted to clear all the lies and let the truth come out. I have hate crawling through my system," she said, when asked why she finally decided to change her story. She felt like confessing would purify her soul and get her right in the eyes of God.

"They got me pissed; hey United States Supreme Court, you fuckin'; I'm telling you man; YOU MOTHERFUCKERS; keep fucking with my god damn execution and there's going to be BLOOD SHED. I'm sick of this—Get that fucking warrent signed." Her frustrations with going back and forth to court, only to be read the same verdict time and time again, had finally hit rock bottom. She was ready to die, and so her time spent going to appeals came to an abrupt end. Aileen really saw no wrong in what she did. She actually felt like she did the cops a service by killing those men, before they had the chance to abuse any other hookers.

"You sabotaged my ass, society. And the cops, and the system—a raped woman got executed. It was used for books and movies and shit. You're an inhumane bunch of fuckin' livin' bastards and bitches and you're gonna get your asses nuked in the end, and pretty soon it's comin'. 2019 a rock's supposed to hit you anyhow, you're all gonna get nuked. You don't take fuckin' human life like this and just sabotage it and rip it apart like Jesus on the cross, and say thanks a lot for all the fuckin' money I made off of ya. And not care about a human being, and the truth being told. Now I know what Jesus was going through."

Chapter Six

Friends or Foes?

While Aileen awaited her sentencing a woman by the name of Arlene Pralle wrote her a letter. She said she had been sent into Aileen's life by God, to guide and comfort her during her most difficult time. Pralle, 44 at the time, wiggled her way in and got closer to Wuornos. She visited her once a week, every week, and talked to her on the phone every night. They even exchanged letters in between visits and phone calls. Pralle was adopted as a child herself, so she understands a little of what life was like for Aileen. However, Pralle was adopted and raised by parents that were well off. She and her husband own a 35-acre farm in Tennessee where they breed Walking Horses. In 1981, Pralle attempted to take her own life as well. Another similarity between her and Aileen. After that, she became a "born again Christian" and changed her entire life around. Not long after that did she run across Wuornos' picture in the newspaper. Pralle says she stared at the woman in the photo for so long it was like her eyes started to speak to her. And that was when she made the decision to reach out to the accused serial killer.

Her first words to Aileen were, "I don't care if you're guilty or not, I want to be your friend." By that point in her life, Wuornos had been so used to being abandoned and alone, she felt like Pralle just may have been sent to her by God, as she herself had also become a born again Christian while incarcerated. Wuornos was hard up for love more than ever after Tyria turned on her, so she let Pralle in.

The women kept in contact the majority of Wuornos' prison bid. She and her husband actually legally adopted Aileen while she was on the inside. It is speculated that the only reason Arlene wanted to be a part of Aileen's life was for the money. There were a lot of books, movies, and documentaries being produced centered around Aileen's case, all which were bringing in a lot of profits. Aileen would never be able to reap any of those benefits, because of the Son of Sam Law held up in Florida, but Arlene figured she could if she were to adopt Wuornos before she was executed. Arlene insists that her only reasoning for adopting a then 35-year-old Lee, was pure love. However, in phone calls

56

and letters with Aileen there had been some talk about her and her husband being able to pay off their farm with the proceeds. I too, share that same belief. However, Pralle held up her duty as Aileen's mother to the public eye by showing off Aileen's more sensitive and kiddush side. She always read her poetry during interviews and showed off the different pictures she drew while in prison.

Believing that Arlene was really in her corner for the right reasons, Aileen wrote her a poem called "Friendship." It reads: "A friend is one who fights to the end to make things right/Our pact as a friend/Cheering you up, never bringing you down/And making sure your life is safe and sound."

Robert Pralle, Arlene Pralle's husband, spoke out about his concerns for his wife's interaction with a serial killer. He was completely against her actions in the beginning, in fear of losing his job, public backlash, and also the constantly piling phone debt she'd accumulated by taking so many collect calls from the prison. It didn't take much for his wife to convince him that she was doing the right thing. He loved and trusted her judgement and agreed to become Aileen's legal father. He also stated that he saw a softer side to Aileen as well. "Outside of her accused crimes, she has a heart of gold," he said.

According to Arlene, becoming the mother of an adult woman accused of being a sadistic, psychopathic serial killer, was really tough. She got a lot of heat from the press. There were always reporters lurking around her farm trying to engage her and her husband in interviews. Arlene had also picked up Aileen's legal fees, the whole nine. She did her best to fight back and bite the bullet most times, though there were a few times where she lost her cool. Especially with Wuornos' legal team and National Feminist Phyllis Chesler, who pushed the idea that Pralle was only in it for the money. It didn't help that her farm business was doing very poorly at the time, and her husband was still living in Chicago. Nonetheless, Arlene and Robert Pralle stood their ground and upheld their claim to love and care for Aileen. "We just want her to have a real family and know that someone loves her," they said.

As time grew on, Aileen herself started to grow suspicious of the Pralles' real intentions with her and her story. There started being more talk about gaining the proceeds from the book and movie publications than actually helping Aileen choose the right route to go about her appeals. Even the phone calls and visits slowed up, and yet again, Aileen found herself alone with no one in her corner. Wuornos went on record to tell interviewers how Arlene and Robert wanted her to plead guilty to all charges. She says that Arlene told her it was time for her to get right with God, and let the healing be done. Wuornos even offered up the information on their suggestions of ways for her to kill herself in prison, because they felt like it would help them get their hands on whatever money was left to Aileen after she was gone. It took Wuornos a while to see the Pralles for who they really were. She was of course upset to learn them, but betrayal was something she had grown accustomed to and till this very day, Arlene and Robert Pralle insist that they were on Aileen's side for all the right reasons.

Dawn Botkins was Aileen's only true friend. She couldn't recall how they met, but figured it must have been through Lori, Aileen's sister, and Keith, her brother. They all hung out together as kids. She remembered the kids saying she had to meet the chick who had a baby, and that Aileen was a prostitute. Dawn didn't even know what a prostitute was until she met Aileen. When Dawn got kicked out of school at 14, Aileen dropped out not long after. They slept in cars together as children. Hitchhiked to the race tracks where Aileen taught Dawn how to "short change." They even ran away together all the way to California. Dawn says they had some pretty scary experiences on the road, but Aileen always made her feel safe. She even had Aileen's ashes sprinkled about her home in Michigan. She never judged Aileen. She loved her for what she saw on the inside and their friendship grew even thicker after Wuornos was incarcerated. When she heard that Aileen was all over the news for murder, she looked her up and kept in constant contact up until the day she was executed. She even went to the prison for visits and also attended the execution.

Botkins didn't even like talking about the murders with Aileen, or anyone. She hated hearing all the bad press and foul words being spewed towards Wuornos, it made her sick. She did everything she could to keep her judgments out of their friendship, because she knew she wouldn't have been able to continue being friends with Wuornos if she hadn't and she didn't want to lose her childhood best friend. She'd always been on Aileen's defense team. Even as children. She was the only one who believed her about being raped as a child. She stood by her when she came home after giving birth, when no one else would. And while she doesn't condone Aileen's actions, she continued to stand by her side and be there for her in her time of need. Something Aileen had always been deprived of from the very beginning.

Dawn talked about testifying in Aileen's defense. There wasn't much she could do, other than testify to Wuornos' character and hard life. Even Aileen's sister, Lori, considered taking the stand right after Dawn. However, Lori got money hungry. She was approached by Jackie Giroux, an English Professor, and promised a payout if she wouldn't share Aileen's story with anyone but her. There were a few other payout promises made to others that knew Aileen growing up, but none of it was ever paid. Dawn and Lori got into many blow-up arguments about her arrangement to sell Aileen's story. Dawn felt like it was wrong, considering Lori and Aileen were sisters, but then again, they never really had a relationship as children. Aileen was an outsider in their family, and she stayed an outsider until the day she died. Dawn was furious by that.

It wasn't her own family who had reached out to Aileen's attorneys, it was Dawn. The minute she saw Aileen on the news, she wrote her attorneys a letter asking to be brought up to speed on the case. They never returned her letter or gave her a call. Finally, out of the blue one day, Trisha Jenkins and Don Sanchez went to visit Dawn to talk about taking the stand. She was eager to do it. She wanted to let the world know what a horrible life Aileen had as a child, and also enlighten them about her real character. Despite her many outbursts and terrible behavior, Dawn says Aileen had a good heart. She even went so far as to borrow a nice dress from a boutique so that Aileen would be proud to see that she had friends who could be seen as respectable.

Dawn hadn't been called to the stand though. No one knows why. Her role was to discredit any lies told by Barry and Lori, against Aileen. Her brother and sister, also dubbed her aunt and uncle, testified that Aileen's life wasn't as hard as she made it to be. The brother/sister duo say she was never abused, raped, or treated unfairly by their father. But, Dawn swears by a different version. She says she witnessed the torture her friend went through and she was ready to spill it all. Maybe she wasn't called to the stand because Wuornos wanted the death penalty? No one knows, and her lawyers never spoke out about why they had gone to see her, but not use her. The only statements made about Dawn not being called to the defense were "Dawn's testimony would not be "earth-shaking." And "it was to protect Aileen."

There were several interviews and TV offers Dawn declined to take on because she thought she was going to be called to the stand to testify. She says she regrets not taking on any of them. She wished she had talked to every single reporter or interviewer and told Aileen's real story. Botkins didn't think the jury would give Wuornos the death penalty if they knew all the details of her life.

Dawn wished she was able to take the stand. She kept track of Barry's testimony and spoke about all the lies he told. He painted his father out to be a nice man who had taken in his grandchildren as his own and gave them a better life. However, Dawn swears that isn't the truth. She even sent a notarized letter to Aileen's defense team that read:

"I know for a fact that Barry Wuornos lied under oath that he was there for Aileen. He indeed was not, for she stayed at my house with Keith and Lori because they were not allowed to stay at their grandfather's house. Except Lori could. And when they were not staying at my house, they were sleeping in cars. I know. I was there. Barry was not there then and is not there now and will never be there for her. He should be ashamed of himself the way he did not take care of Aileen and Keith... he treated her like shit just like everybody else did."

Botkins says she has a lot to thank Aileen for. Much like a few of her friends who worked at the biker bars in Daytona, the place Wuornos called home. Dawn remembers a time where Aileen took her to the mall and bought her purse and everything that women carry in purses. She says she was never the type to carry purses, but since her friend insisted she have one, she let her buy it. Those were the kinds of memories Dawn wished the jury could have heard about Aileen. She wasn't the monster the media made her out to be, in Dawn's eyes. There were even times where Aileen would give all of the money she made from prostituting to the homeless. "She really had a good heart," Dawn says. She even thanks Aileen for finding her husband. They were hitchhiking when Dawn met the love of her life, a man named Dave. They have a beautiful home in Michigan, and beautiful children. Something Dawn never thought she would have if it weren't for being on the road with Aileen.

There were times where Dawn felt guilty for not being able to save her friend. She even stayed up some nights and cried about it. When Arlene came into Aileen's life, Dawn was the first one to become suspicious. At first, she felt like maybe she was just jealous because she had been Aileen's best friend their whole life, and in came someone new. She was ok with Pralle adopting Aileen, because it seemed to keep Aileen in good spirits, but she still carried her doubts about the woman. Soon her doubts were all confirmed when she got several letters from prison expressing Aileen's concerns about her adopted mother. In one letter in particular she gave Dawn some real feedback on what she felt Arlene, and the police, were cheating and lying about. The moment she started seeing the woman didn't actually stand for what she claimed she stood for, all hell broke loose. The cops had her taken to medical lockdown and to her knowledge "pumped her full of drugs" because they wanted to keep her in the state of mind that she was in when she was first arrested. Tranquilized. She says she was already detoxing from all the alcohol she had been consuming, and the drugs only made it worse for her. The drug and alcohol detox pills, on top of the pills she was given to treat her anxiety, made her fall into a slumber.

Fifteen days had passed, and Aileen was still in medical lockup. She learned that the pills given to her had been prescribed by Arlene's personal doctor and grew furious because she felt as though she had no say over what was going into her body. When a person becomes an inmate, or ward of the state, unless they are analyzed and treated by the state's doctor, family members may have medicine brought in for them as long as it is prescribed by a doctor and the prescription is brought along with it. Being that Arlene was Aileen's legal guardian, she was able to have her put on meds with, or without, Aileen's consent. She says,

63

"once I became hooked on the drugs, they let me out." She really believed she had been purposely drugged, so when she went to court she would appear to be incompetent, all because Aileen wanted the proceeds from the book and movie offers. According to her, that was the first thing ever brought up in conversation when her "public pretender" came to visit her after her fifteen-day medical stay. Stunned by his words, Aileen quickly stated she wasn't interested in any book or movie deals, she wanted to know what was going on with her case. There was no way she wanted to spend the rest of her life in prison.

By the words in her letter, she was shocked. Completely taken by surprise. In her mind she had really murdered seven men in self-defense. She says her concerns were ignored and Cass, her public defender, reminded her that she had no financial family to help keep her up while she was in prison. He said that his main concern, at that time, was to help her financially. Again, she told him that she wasn't interested in any of that, and he left. Cass returned two days later with an old friend of Aileen's. Russel Armstrong, another public defender who had defended her back in 1981 when she was in the hot seat for armed robbery. For a moment, Aileen grew excited thinking that he was going to be taking over her case, but that didn't happen. Cass had merely brought in a familiar face because he thought it might help Aileen change her mind about the movie deal. He told her that he would take care of all the legal responsibilities for her in that area, and he wouldn't even charge her to do it. After thinking about what she could possibly gain, and a very persuading conversation, she finally changed her mind and agreed to have the movies and books put into the works.

Wuornos says that Armstrong and Cass made sure she knew that they could lose their jobs behind making a deal like that, so she had to keep everything quiet. They didn't want her to talk about the movie to anyone at all. That was very suspicious to her. She even says that Jackie, the woman responsible for the content of the movie, was willing to give Aileen sixty dollars a month until the movie was completed. To a woman who had no one on the outside to help foot the bills in prison, that seemed like a great contract.

That's where the beef with Arlene really started. Because of the Son of Sam Law, Aileen was told that her money had to be put into a trust fund. Legally, she wasn't able to touch any of the money, but her legal guardian, Arlene, as well as her lawyers, would handle the money and send her any amount she requested, whenever she requested it. Once the movie was finished, she started to ask for the money, but no one ever sent her a dime. Arlene even stopped answering calls and coming to visit.

Chapter Seven

A Feminist's Analysis

Phyllis Chesler had behind-the-scenes access to Aileen Wuornos. Phyllis is a feminist leader, a psychotherapist, and expert courtroom witness. She wanted to testify in Aileen's defense, and point out the dangers and traumas that are very well involved with being a prostitute, especially for someone as young as Aileen was when she started selling her body. In one of her books she goes on to say that the bullets Aileen used to kill all of those men were to shatter the silence of the violence that women endure during prostitution. So, in a way, she actually deemed Aileen as sort of an advocate for female prostitutes. Which I'm sure a lot of women could see the sense in. Chesler says her involvement in the case and wants to help Wuornos stemmed from a single question. "Does a prostitute have the right to defend her own life?" Her answer was, "Probably not." And it's somewhat agreeable. There have been dozens of cases where prostitutes have claimed to be sexually assaulted and just because their line of work is "sex work" no one believes them. Especially the police. A lot of sex-working women would rather settle the score on their own rather than go to the police, because they know it'll be a dead-end street.

Phyllis believes Aileen suffered from battered women's syndrome, a psychological condition developed by women after long-term abuse, and it is easily defendable. Look at the way she was raised. The way she was treated by her own family members and guys her age in the schoolyard. She never stood a chance at life. Even her own father had been diagnosed with a mental illness and it's not hard to believe that she suffered from the same illness. On top of that, she was already considered a criminal, so she wouldn't risk going to the police and being sent away for life, for murder. When asked about why none of her expert witnesses were ever called to testify by the defense, Phyllis stated that Aileen's public defender, Trish Jenkins, would never sit down and talk with her. Aileen practically had to order her to take an interview and afterwards, Phyllis learned that the extent of Trish's experience was defending male rapists and male serial killers. Lee was also the most difficult client Trish had ever had to defend. She didn't know how to save herself, thus making it harder for everyone else to try and help save her. Wuornos was very well experienced in how to take care of herself and survive living on the streets, her mind just couldn't understand why other women who understood her lifestyle would ever want to try and help her with her hearing. She either didn't trust them, or was afraid of being hurt again and didn't want to let anyone else get close to her.

If her public defender would have called some of the expert feminist witness team that Phyllis had put together, Aileen would have at least had a fighting chance on one of her cases. The jury would have also gotten the chance to learn about other cases where women, prostitutes just like Aileen, argued self-defense in similar cases and actually won. They never got to hear the phrase "Self-defense," which is unbelievable because Aileen blurted it out from the very beginning. She even uttered it a whopping 16 times in her confession video. The court didn't care that one of the grounds for appeal was the non-calling of any expert witness. They upheld Aileen's sentence anyway. It was also overlooked that Richard Mallory, the first victim of Wuornos, was high as a kite the night of his murder. He was also addicted to porn, and could have easily done all of the things Aileen claimed he had. Still, no expert witnesses were called in Aileen's defense to testify. Mallory had a long history of violence towards women, hence why he spent ten years in a federal prison. If either of those facts had been brought up in court, Wuornos could have easily beaten her case vs. Mallory. Wuornos had been advised to carry a gun by men she had befriended, after her run-in with Mallory.

With an already troubled past, and possible mental health issues, Aileen put her own practices into effect after her incident with Richard Mallory. And if a guy wanted to do things she didn't want to, even if there was money involved, if they got too demanding, or rough, she killed them. No questions asked. That was her understanding of why she had the gun in the first place. Her level of comprehension did not exceed past the grade in which she dropped out of school. Some even questioned her competency there. A lot of things were uncoordinated in Aileen's mind, and that's something that an expert witness, being a female feminist, could have helped get across to the jury.

Aileen's right to a fair trial was not practiced at all. She was labeled as a lesbian prostitute who hated men, none of those people in the jury box were her peers. They were all churchgoers, law and order watchers, or retired Floridians with old-school practices. Her entire trial was biased from the very beginning. Aileen didn't fit in with them, so it was easy for them to look at her crimes and immediately want her erased from their world. There wasn't a single prostitute on her jury. Not one person who came from the same type of background as Aileen. There weren't even any female advocates on her jury. It was designed to have her thrown to the wolves and judged based off of what type of lifestyle she lived. Also, in Florida, once you say you that you oppose the death penalty, you're supposed to be removed from jury duty. That wasn't put into effect either. To add even more weight to Aileen's shoulders, the prosecutor, John Tanner, had a very negative outlook towards prostitutes. He stated himself, in several articles he'd written, that he believed they were the cause of so many men having AIDS and HIV. In fact, studies show that it's actually the opposite. It could have easily been argued that Tanner went after Wuornos so hard not only because she was a woman, but she was also a prostitute.

The fight in the end ultimately came down to gender and prostitution. The jury in Aileen's case had never once been educated on what the effects were of a woman who had been prostituting for more than 20 years, or what it meant for her whenever one of her johns got too physical. A woman could never know what a man will do to her in that situation, and she would only be left with a split second to make a decision on how she would defend herself. Expert witnesses could have pointed that out to the jury as well. They were never put in the position to have to ask themselves how they would react if it were them, or one of their loved ones in that situation. All that was drilled into their heads was that Wuornos was a menace to society.

Although Wuornos actually wanted the death penalty, if jurors had been educated on the life of prostitution, they may have found her guilty, but not recommended the death penalty. They also should have only been focused on the first murder, rather than all seven murders at once, in the Mallory case. They could have never believed that Aileen acted out of self-defense with Richard Mallory, because they had already been told about the other murders. They were already biased towards her claim of self-defense based on that alone.

It is to be believed that Wuornos was beyond human grace. There was no way for her to be saved. Even if her first claim of self-defense was

70

true. She was a monster, and she knew that to be true herself. There was some sort of chemical imbalance in her brain; look at her father. The life she was born into and all of the dysfunction she and her family had gone through. She may have indeed had a good side to her, but unfortunately her bad side outweighed all of her good judgement. There was no way for Aileen to be salvaged. She was too far gone and to her own discretion, did not want to be reeled in. She enjoyed her life. What little life she had, and in the end she was ok with finally letting herself go. She wanted to be with God. The only man she saw that would truly love her and never leave her side.

She wasn't like most male serial killers and certainly nothing like any female serial killers. Lee was very different. There are tons of women who have been brought up the same exact way as she had been, but not all of them turn to the same life of crime that Aileen had. Many of them run away from home, turn to prostitution, and even get involved with petty and, or violent crimes, but not all of them become serial killers. Wuornos killed male strangers. And they were all big guys, some of them had even been involved in law enforcement at some point in their lives. For Wuornos, there had to have been some kind of a thrill, other than just the money. She was indeed strapped for cash, but there were other ways to go about getting some than killing her johns. Something she knew as well, being that she had once married a man for his riches, and even held up a mini-mart at gunpoint.

Severe, prolonged, childhood trauma plays a huge part in the background of a lot of serial killers. Even some non-serial killers have a traumatic past. The thinking patterns in these instances become very corrupt. They start to think about things that they would normally never even consider. It stems from the abuse they endure, studies have shown. Oftentimes, when people grow up in certain environments, they start to believe that the way they were raised is the norm. For most of us we know better than to believe a lot of the negatives that we say, but for victims of abuse, like Wuornos, they really believe that their lives are normal. In several interviews, Wuornos is seen and heard talking about her victims like they were nothing. It was almost as if none of her wrongdoings were actually wrong. She really believed that she was in the right and that she should suffer no consequences for what she had done, because the men she killed were already doing something wrong. That was the way her grandfather treated her throughout her entire life. Not only him, but her real peers as well.

Crime and violence became her way of relating to "normal" people. Unfortunately, not everyone was brought up the same way that Aileen had been brought up, and she encountered a lot of sneers and backlash for a lot of her actions, things that she felt were normal. Not just her killings. And people were so afraid of her because of how quick and hot her temper was, no one wanted to take the time out to teach her anything different. Tyria tried to, at one point, but even she, Aileen's most beloved, had grown tired of the outbursts, and even more afraid of her, and washed her hands clean of Aileen and their relationship. Violence, in a sense, was the way that Aileen showed love. It was all she knew from a very young age and it stuck with her up until the day that she was executed, in a Florida state prison, for the robberies and murders of seven men. She claimed self-defense in all seven cases.

Wuornos was essentially getting revenge for all the times she had been abused as a child. That's the way she saw things from her perspective. Oftentimes female children who have been sexually abused don't value themselves and their bodies. That was Aileen. She felt like since no one else respected her and her body, why should she. So, even though she was getting paid to have sexual relations with the men she murdered, in her eyes they were still taking advantage of her because she was a prostitute. She was basically repeating the trauma over and over again, and eventually it became exhausting and unbearable.

When you have really unhealthy relationships, it is fairly easy to develop a borderline personality disorder. The world around you becomes so chaotic, especially for Wuornos. She never had any real bonds with people. She had her brother Keith and her grandmother, but even their relationships had their dark sides. Especially with her brother. Her best friend, Dawn, did her best to show Aileen unconditional love and for the most part she did, however, Aileen could never sit still long enough to take it all in.

Nick Broomfield, Wuornos' favorite reporter, pointed out that she was mentally unfit for execution. No one believed him. He replayed his footage from their interviews and rewatched several instances where Aileen rambled about eating poisoned food, and even the police being involved with at least one of her murders. Of course, Wuornos claimed she was mentally fit and actually wanted to be executed, but Broomfield, as well as other outsiders looking in, believed otherwise. It isn't hard to see in her interviews that she's mentally unstable, and it was also later determined that she did suffer from borderline personality disorder, as well as PTSD.

Wuornos' recognizable mugshot and cracked smile had become the face of female evil in the world. On the outside, she appears to be this gun-slinging monster with a ruthless outlook on life. To some, she had become a serious cult hero. Oddly. During her trial, Aileen stated, "*I killed those men. Robbed them as cold as ice. And I'd do it again, too. There's no chance in keeping me alive or anything, because I'd kill again. I have hate crawling through my system...I am so sick of hearing this 'she's crazy' stuff. I've been evaluated so many times. I'm competent, sane, and I'm trying to tell the truth. I'm one who seriously hates human life and would kill again.*"

There was a moment in court where Aileen thought the cameras were off and she was heard muttering that she only told the courts she intended to kill those men because she wanted their money, but it was really all out of self-defense. She wanted to die. She hated the thought of spending the rest of her days in prison, so death row was the way she wanted to go out. Aileen hated people. She could be seen laughing and smiling with a few of the prison guards from time to time, but there was a burning hatred for people deep down in her soul that she just couldn't get rid of.

Wuornos was interviewed one last time, a day before her execution. She appeared to be happy and content, ready to get it over with. She even stated that she was alright with it. She had made her peace with God and was ready to go home. Finally. Aileen was so out of it by the time it was time for her to be executed, she believed that prison guards had an intercom placed inside her cell and used "sonic pressure" to play tricks with her mind. She stated that every time she would try to write something the sound waves would go up higher, causing her to suffer from chronic headaches. There was a huge satellite on the prison compound that Aileen believed was rigged to the TV or the mirrors in her cell. She said there was an electrician who put the mirror on the wall and he supposedly asked her if it looked like a computer to her. She said the sonic pressure from the mirrors, TV, and intercom were set in place to crush her head. Every time she brought it up to the prison warden, she said they increased the pressure. She constantly complained about the conditions in prison. Her food was inedible. The intercoms were crushing her head. Her mirrors were rigged. She was being tortured and made to look like she was crazy, when in fact, she was crazy. She just didn't believe that she was. It is quite possible that Aileen's borderline personality disorder played a part in all of this. On one side of her brain she very well may have been perfectly sane, but on the other side there was that darkness. One that she had no control over and no one aided to contain. In her last days she truly believed the police were out to make her look crazy so no one believed anything she had to say.

As for her execution, Aileen described it as a recolonization to another planet, or like Star Trek beaming her up to the beyond. She believed God and all the angels would be there watching over her, waiting for her to be done to go home with them. She was nearly ecstatic about it. She had no fear whatsoever, and no remorse for what she had done to her victims. She said she did the right thing by killing each of those men, so she knew that wherever she would end up after her death would be an amazing place. In a way, she believed she saved a lot of other women from being raped and killed by her seven victims.

During her last interview she was asked if she had anything she wanted to say about the cops who arrested her. She stated, "A LOT OF STUFF." She desperately wanted it to be known that the cops were watching her while she killed those men, and that she knew it. She said that police had helicopters dropping down from the sky with decoys to pick her up 4 to 5 months before she was finally arrested. To her, she was sent down to "clean up the streets."

Aileen had been a victim her entire life, so it was easy for her to believe that the whole world was out to get her. It was the norm for her to think that no one ever really loved her. Once she became an adult, life just became so unbearable for her that she spiraled completely out of control. She lashed out on everyone, almost as though she was protecting the inner child of hers that no one ever protected. Several studies have shown that Wuornos was born a psychopath. Her triggers from being abused is what set her off and drove her to kill.

Chapter Eight

Case Examination

S tage One: Initial response. This is where a crime is reported. It's always the first step into an investigation. The crime can be reported by phone, an eyewitness bringing information to the police station, a link from another crime, or crimes. In Wuornos' case the initial response would be the findings of all her victims. The first step is always the most important step. Investigators will gather all evidence, clues, and links and proceed with caution. If the crime is not reported to the police, there can be no investigation. Crimes always have to be reported before there can be any justice. In Richard Mallory's case, detectives decided to investigate because the truck being abandoned looked suspicious. There was visible blood inside the truck, which gave them probable cause to search. However, being that there were no victims, perps, or witnesses, backup was not needed on the scene at the time. If either the victim, perp, or witness would have been present at the scene it would have been the officers' duty to report and investigate. What made Mallory's truck a different circumstance was the blood behind the steering wheel. Officers felt like that was suspicious enough to report and therefore sparked a full-on investigation. Twelve days later a body was discovered, and after further investigation they found out that it was in fact Richard Mallory.

As for David Spears, the investigation started out much the same. Police found an abandoned truck and felt like the scene was suspicious, though it has never been disclosed as to how the truck was found. After calling for further assistance to determine whether or not there was anything that needed to be investigated. There were no victims, perps, or witnesses left behind, so there was no need for further investigation at that time. Twelve days later, his body was discovered, sparking the investigation.

Charles Carskadon's body was found and his abandoned vehicle found a day later. There are no documents that state whether the police found the body, or a member of the general public, just that his deceased body was found. Her lawyers could have argued this fact during her trial, to further back up her statements that she was set up, but it was never mentioned.

In the case of Peter Siems, the only investigation that had been done was the one on his car. Police got a call about a car accident. There were no victims, or perps present, but there was an eyewitness. The woman described what she had seen, as well as the two women involved. Her report, the presence of blood inside the vehicle, and the discovery of who the car belonged to sparked the investigation into Peter Siems. His body was never found.

Eugene Burress' wife reported him missing a week before his work truck had been discovered with the keys missing. There was no sign of a struggle, no blood, or a body at the time, so there wasn't much investigating that could be done. His body was found badly decomposed not long after.

Although there was no date stated in reports, it is stated that Charles Humphreys' wife had also reported him missing before his body was found. Another fact Wuornos' lawyers could have argued during her trial. However, with several murders already on file, carrying the same MO and the same style, police started their search for Humphreys immediately. Not long after, his body was found. His car was found abandoned days later.

A police officer reported the findings of Walter Gino Antonio. It hasn't been stated as to how he happened to come across the body, but in this case it doesn't matter. There was already an investigation spiraling around these crimes that were presumably connected, so there was no need for an initial response in this case. His car was found abandoned not long after. Whether by police or civilian has not been stated.

In Aileen's defense, there were some loopholes in her case and they all began at the initial response stage. As stated before, the initial response is crucial to all investigations, because without that initial response to the crime, there can be no investigation. It's almost as if the crime doesn't exist, until someone calls it in. If Wuornos had had lawyers on her side that were not working for the state, she may have been seen in a different light to the jurors. Even if she hadn't been seen in a different light, she may have had her case tried more fairly.

Preliminary Investigations: the second stage. This is where investigators section off the crime scene, collect their evidence, and also witness statements. They take pictures of the scene, log anything that looks like it's related to the crime, take video footage and everything in between. That way, when and if they catch their suspect, they have all their ducks in a row that show why this person should be held accountable. It is vital that this step is taken with precaution. If there is any evidence on the scene that is overlooked, tampered with, or cross contaminated, they cannot be used in court. And oftentimes, lack of evidence is grounds for release of a suspect. The victims in Wuornos' case were all found in areas that weren't heavily trafficked, therefore any evidence found on the scenes were intact enough to hold up in future court proceedings.

At Richard Mallory's crime scene it was very evident that there was more than one person on the scene at the commission of the crime. Pictures were immediately taken of the scene and surrounding area, before any evidence was lifted from the victim or the surrounding area. What made investigators believe that there were two people at the scene was the bottle of alcohol and two cups discarded near the scene. Mallory's driver's license was also discovered on the scene. Investigators also made note that it seemed as if the driver's seat had been adjusted for someone smaller to drive the car. All crucial factors to the case. Upon more thorough investigation, it was noted that there was an indentation of a tool box left in the trunk of the car, but there was no tool box. Future investigations revealed that Wuornos had pawned Mallory's tools. The vehicle had been dusted for fingerprints at the scene, but there were none. Wuornos was smart enough to keep Windex in her "kill bag" and carefully wipe away any traces of herself she may have left behind. It has been speculated that the technique used to test for fingerprints wasn't executed properly, though it's never been stated which technique was actually used. The vehicle was later transported and investigated further for any missed evidence.

When called to investigate the crime scene of David Spears, detectives found a single hair and an open pack of condoms in the vehicle. There was also other "suspicious" evidence and belongings of David's found. The owner of the vehicle had been determined by the vin number, as there were no fingerprints or other forms of DNA available at the time. Investigators also noted that the driver's seat had been adjusted to suit a person much smaller than David. The only collected evidence from the crime scene was a used condom, the packet it came from, and several cans of beer. Which made police suspect that David was not alone at the time of the incident. David's body was later transported for further analysis, where he had been identified through his dental records.

Charles Carskadon's crime scene didn't produce as much evidence as the others. The findings reported were some of his personal belongings, like clothes and a shaving kit, and also a .45 caliber pistol. Prosecutors have stated that Wuornos actually pawned a .45 and that was where they discovered another of her fingerprints, but it is questioned because of the evidence findings log.

For the accident in Peter Siems' car, there was a witness statement taken at the scene. The surrounding areas were searched for any other clues relating to the crash. There was note of what appeared to be blood in the vehicle, as well as numerous cans of beer found at the site of the crash. All of these factors would have been taken into account in order to find out who the perp, or victim was.

Detectives actually found documents relating to where Eugene Burress worked on the scene of his crime. Therefore, it wasn't hard to identify his body. Burress' wife also identified him by his wedding ring. His deceased body was transported to medical examiners, who determined the cause of death to be homicide. Two wounds from a .22 caliber pistol were located in his upper torso, much like the bodies before him.

Miscellaneous items were taken from the scene of Charles Humphreys' murder. Things like his ID. Empty beer cans found near the car. It has never been cleared up why, but detectives chose not to process any fingerprints from the beer cans. His body was later transported to medical examiners, who determined his cause of the death to be the same as prior victims.

Police did, however, dust for fingerprints on beer cans found at the scene of Walter Gino Antonio. Maybe the officers in Antonio's county were more thorough with their investigation, or maybe officers in Charles Humphreys' county felt like fingerprints weren't necessary in their case, because they had enough to go on from the cases in other counties. There were no fingerprints found on the can in Antonio's case. Wuornos' lawyers could have argued there was a lack of evidence, in connection with Humphreys' case—since the prosecution felt the need to run all the cases together. However, his body was transported to medical examiners and the cause of death was determined to be gunshot wounds from a .22 caliber pistol.

Stage Three: Planning the investigation. This is also an important factor when planning to bring down justice. Investigators need to carefully plan how they will pull off the investigation, without getting their suspect/suspects spooked, or giving out too much information about the investigation to the public. Authorities may want to ensure the public that they are doing what needs to be done to solve the crime, but also keeping their investigation under tight wraps, as it can be easy to miss the target if too much information is given right away. There is also a follow-up investigation process.

Stage Four: This is where police revisit evidence taken from the crime scenes, witness statements, and family members to check for new information. They also gather information from any forensic tests, officers in other counties, as well as tips from anonymous hotlines. There have been a lot of cases solved just off tips from the public alone. In Wuornos' case, fingerprints from the victims' pawned valuables and witness testimony is what brought her into the investigators' eyesight. Had there been no follow-up investigations, Wuornos might have still been reigning terror on the highways of Florida.

Stage Five: The incident room. Incident rooms are usually set up close to the area where a serious crime has been committed. Officials want to make this location easily accessible to anyone who has further information that may assist with the crime at hand. Sometimes they're set up in public libraries, schools, or town halls. Anywhere the public can get to with information to crack a case. They also have a hotline set up that takes calls 24/7. This stage of the process can be set up at any point during the investigation, so long as it is set up. Incident rooms come in handy whenever officials are at a stand-still within the case being investigated. Sometimes, the community can get a case solved even quicker than the police, and it's all thanks to having somewhere to dump whatever information they know.

There was no incident room set up in Aileen's case. It hasn't been revealed why. It can be speculated that police didn't need any further assistance from the public with their case. With the evidence collected, witness statements, and confirmations from composite sketches, they may have felt as though their case was open and shut. That was all the evidence they needed in order to get Wuornos to sit down for an official interview, where she herself connected the dots for the police.

Stage Six: Investigating leads. It is vital to investigate any leads in any investigation. Leads help determine the route detectives may want to take throughout their investigation. Without properly investigating their leads, they may wind up at a dead end. Or an end that was meant to intentionally distract them from where they needed to be, something Wuornos tried to do by dumping the bodies in a different location than where she abandoned her victims' vehicles.

Leads are also fingerprint evidence, other DNA evidence, witnesses that have been interviewed, as well as those newly coming forth. Police will review any footage available. They visit the homes of their victims and witnesses, and any other homes close to the scene of the crime. This stage is important when trying to identify the suspect. If a suspect is immediately apprehended, this stage can, and oftentimes will be, carried out earlier on in the investigation. However, if all leads are not carefully investigated, it may lead to a suspect being released. In Aileen's case, there were a lot of leads that needed to be followed before she could actually be charged with any murders. There were the fingerprints found on some of the beer cans from different scenes. The witnesses who were interviewed by police. Callers who were able to identify her from the sketch photos, and also the motive of the crime. Police believed their killer was either motivated by sex, or the need to rob their victim. All of the crimes had the same MO, but all of their leads still needed to be properly investigated on their own in order to legally try the case.

Stage Seven: Research and analysis. In this stage of the investigation police take all things into consideration. Evidence. Witness statements. Current crime trends in the area, in order to see who's committing what types of crimes so they can rule out suspects. Research and analysis was very essential in Aileen's case. There were several victims, all murdered in the same fashion. All of their cars and bodies were found discarded in the same manner, except for one body. The conclusions of researching and analyzing each victim's lifestyles, patterns and routines, their friends and families, it became evident to the police that they were all being picked up by the same person. A hooker. Without that research it may have been a little harder for police to link all of the crimes together, as the number of bodies grew fairly quickly.

Stage Eight: Gathering and analyzing the facts. This is where the overview takes place. Police regroup and do a review of everything they've learned about the case with the goal of ensuring they have covered all of their tracks. They ensure that all forensics evidence was properly gathered and stored, so there is no waste or cross contamination, and also to ensure that it will in fact hold up in court. If all the proper steps are taken correctly, it enables detectives to be able to pinpoint the suspect and also the motive for the crimes. If evidence is ever gathered incorrectly, it is grounds for release of the suspect.

Detectives used several different methods of analyzing the facts in Wuornos' case. All of the evidence collected from the scenes of the crimes were used as facts in her trial. Even several witness statements were used. Ballistics evidence from the bullets she loaded her gun with were also used to form the conclusion. The fingerprints from Peter Siems' car being a match to Wuornos and the false identification used to pawn off his stolen goods were key in cracking the case.

Stage Nine: Identifying patterns and links. If there are crimes in different states, or counties, detectives will try to gather as much information as they can from each of the crimes to determine if there is any relevance. They share what they know of the crimes from their jurisdiction with other agencies and come together to make the conclusion of whether or not the crimes are serial.

The patterns were discovered late in Aileen's case. Her style of murder really threw the police off. They were under the assumption that their killer had to be a male, because it wasn't popular for a woman to commit serial murders in the way that Aileen had. This stage of the investigation was another crucial point in Wuornos' case. The patterns shown in each individual case was the age and gender of the victims. The caliber of the pistol. The number of shots fired into the same area of each victim. The way the driver's seat was adjusted in each vehicle. The robbery of each victim. And also the way their bodies were found, naked. There were a lot of other similarities in each individual case, and the analysis of the patterns played a major role in helping police identify their suspect.

Stage Ten: Process of elimination. This stage of the investigation can also be executed early on, if there is significant evidence showing the innocence of anyone who may have been involved in the crime committed. Each witness in Wuornos' cases were carefully analyzed and eventually eliminated as suspects, because of the significant evidence found pointing to Wuornos.

Stage Eleven: Ethical considerations. In this stage, officials use the press, media, and other public news outlets to further assist with their investigation. However, it must be taken into grave consideration, as it could also hinder any further investigations. The family members of the victims are also considered here. It has to be a thought in the minds of investigators to protect the victims and their families, as well as any witnesses, from further harm. For instance, if Aileen had been working with an accomplice and the media came forth with the identities of any witnesses, Wuornos' accomplice may have been out in a position to retaliate on her behalf. There are instances where investigators do not take into consideration the safety of those involved with their case, because they simply want to solve the case, and witnesses have come up missing. Resulting in the release of the criminal.

Stage Twelve: Report writing and presenting evidence to the court. The last step in the investigation happens when the suspect has been arrested and is awaiting sentencing, or trial. The case is prepared for the court after the defense and prosecution touch basis. Every piece of evidence is carefully examined and written into the logs for its presentation in court. Each stage in the investigation is all in preparation for the final stage. The goal in this stage is to charge the correct suspected criminal and bring justice to the crimes at hand. There is also a case file prepared for the courts in this stage. That would include all of Wuornos' previous interactions with law enforcements, whether she had been convicted of her crimes or not. In all seven murder cases, justice prevailed.

Chapter Nine

In Her Own Words

Lee, the name she liked to go by, told a story of the view from inside her cell. It was her only taste of very little freedom. Her view was of the state prison's parking lot, that's it. There were no trees, no nothing. There weren't even any open bars on her cell door. Instead, she was confined behind a steel door. The only mistake she considered she ever made to land her such terrible luck, was prostitution. She wished she never got into that life at all, because it was what led her down such a lonely, dark path in life. She spent the majority of her prison time thinking about writing a book. A book that would tell all of her deepest, darkest secrets. She wanted people to know the real Lee. Not the monster the police and news reporter made her out to be. She also wanted to write about the treatment of the inmates, and the flaws in the system, when it came down to defending the rights of the indigenous people, referring to all public defenders as "public pretenders."

Her daily rounds started at seven o'clock sharp. Every morning. The day always started off with a fresh cup of prison coffee and whatever the guards had agreed to put on the TV. On weekdays, she spent about two hours every morning cleaning up her cell, in case a random cell raid just so happened to be in the cards for her that day. Whenever she would sit to write her letters, or doodle up some postcards to send to Dawn, she sat on her prison-issued pillow and used her storage locker as her desk. Her locker was used for more than just writing. She used it as a table during chow time. She used it as a TV stand for her small personal TV, and even a book shelf to keep her books from being damaged.

11:00 and 4:00 were the times she looked forward to the most. Lunch and dinner, and also the mail ran around those times. Although she wasn't popular in her community, she gained a lot of moral support and sympathy from women who had been in her situation before once her case went viral. They sent her dozens of letters from all over the world. Some good, some bad. Her favorite letters always came from her friend Dawn, back home in Michigan. Her favorite shows were Wheel of Fortune and Jeopardy. She watched the news long enough to see what they were saying about her and turned it off just as quickly as she had put it on. Sometimes, if there was a good movie playing she would retire from her writing and doodling just long enough to pay attention, if not, she would write. That was her most favorite thing to do. It gave her a real peace of mind. She was able to be transparent with herself, and others, about the unfair treatment she felt as though the world handed her all throughout life. And that was what she did every day like clockwork.

Lee met some friends during her time in prison. Judi, Andrea, and Deidre. She met up with them four times a week when she was allowed yard time to keep her sanity and get a few breaths of fresh air. Most times she liked being by herself. That's the way she had grown accustomed to living her life anyway. Also, she would often get into arguments with the women she called "friends" and that wasn't the way she wanted to spend her time. It was bad enough she had to spend it in prison. She was tired of fighting and wanted nothing more than to have peace of mind. For once in her life. While being locked away, Lee really saw herself growing spiritually. Her favorite genre of books to read were all about spiritual growth and human development. Whenever she would finish reading one of the books, she would write a long letter to her adopted mother about what she had taken away from her reading. Her growth showed in her letters too. Before, she could barely get out an understandable sentence, but after reading and learning more about herself through the books, she made a lot of sense. Much more sense than the public made it seem like she had.

Before falling out with her mother, Arlene Pralle, she wrote about how she wished it was possible for them to have an opportunity to spend some time together, without her being incarcerated. Which was something very new, considering her extreme dislike for all human beings. She even considered waiting twenty to thirty years for that opportunity to arise, even though towards the end of her trial she pushed her lawyers to fight for the death penalty because she was so against spending such a lengthy time in prison. Lee felt like when Arlene came into her life and adopted her, and showed her so much love and concern, that she was truly heaven sent. She was even afraid to die before getting the chance to wrap her arms around the woman she grew to call Mom. A drastic change in her feelings considering the way she felt towards the end of her trial.

In a letter written to Dawn, Aileen says she quit writing to Arlene months before she and Dawn made contact again. She says Arlene started to distance herself after she found out that she wouldn't be getting any of the money that was offered up in the beginning to Aileen. Lee believes that the only reason Arlene and her husband adopted her was so they could reap the benefits of her story after she was gone. She says they even conned her into not going to any more of her appeals once she was finally assigned to death row.

Arlene tells a different story about the way she and Lee ended things. She says that when Lee was sentenced to death she grew nasty and hateful towards her. She started to demand money be put into her account and accused everyone trying to render her aid as being deceitful and conspiracists. After she was calmed down she would write again saying that she loved Arlene, but the damage was already done. Arlene says Lee's words felt like manipulation and hurt even more than being abused. She went on to describe Lee as an eight-year-old living in an adult body. Her temper tantrums were the butt of that. Whenever she didn't get her way, is when she got mean and nasty.

Nonetheless, Lee seemed to be in kind spirits whenever she spoke to Dawn. Twenty years had passed since they last saw one another, at Keith's funeral, and Dawn's love for her hadn't changed a bit. The only thing Dawn didn't like about Aileen, was the name "Lee." She never referred to her by that name. Ever. She was also iffy about the position in which Arlene played in Lee's life, but she passed no judgement there either. If Lee was happy with it, she did her best to cope without giving her too much input on the subject. The majority of the time, Dawn would change the subject whenever Lee brought the woman up in conversation.

To the public eye, Tyria was Lee's first female lover. However, in letters to Dawn, Lee revealed that she in fact had a female lover a while before she met Ty. One that she really loved and cared for, but who had also ripped her off. It wasn't until she went looking for a replacement that she ran into Ty and fell in love again. She also expresses in that same letter her frustrations with the world thinking that she was nothing more than a high school dropout with a ninth grade education level. She tells her friend how she studied psychology, theology, the brain, the nervous system, algebra, anatomy, and had even read the Bible in its entirety several times. She did all of this while the world saw her as nothing but a hitch-hiking prostitute. That was where a lot of her anger and frustration came from in her adult years.

She talks about the pain she suffered as a child in her letters. As well as the sadness she endured as a lonely adult over the years. Everyone in her life had betrayed her. Dawn was the only one who stayed true to their roots and true to her words as a friend. She hated being labeled as a serial killer, though she was. In her eyes, a serial killer was a man who stalked and preyed on his victims. She saw herself as merely a woman who "semi" did a good deed in the world. Yes, she was a prostitute, and yes she did kill all of those men, but if there weren't any johns to trick off she would have never been in her position, type of thing. She also made it a point to mention that she had "only" shot those men to death. She believed that real serial killers only committed "brutal" murders and also, their "cooling off" period only lasted a few days. Not months, like hers did.

When she talks about the night she met Richard Mallory, she goes into grave details. She says he raped her. Tied her to his steering wheel and repeatedly rammed his penis into her anal and vaginal canal for nearly two hours. She says he got off on hearing her cry and scream out in agony. Afterwards, she said he cleaned himself up, her as well, with rubbing alcohol he stored inside a Visine bottle, because he didn't want any "hooker" juice being left on him. Lee said she never had anal sex before. She wasn't into all the exotic sex. She just wanted to make her money and go about her business. Her "regulars" as she called them, most of them were in the military fighting in desert storm, which was why she had been meeting up with so many strangers.

She believed no one bought her self-defense claim because of all the buzz her case had gotten before it was even tried. She says their idea for the movie was completely false and didn't match up to anything she told detectives during her confession. She also says that Tyria's testimony was a lie as well. Lee believed that Tyria had either been paid off with the promises of proceeds from the books and movie deals, or she had turned on her in order to keep herself from doing a bid with her. Because Tyria knew all along about the murders and had never gone to the police. In fact, Lee says that it was Tyria's idea for her to keep doing what she was doing to keep bringing in the money.

When she recollected the time of her confession, she says she badgered. The cops had already made their minds up about her before they even let her tell her story. She said that every time she tried to tell them about the rapes, they cut her off with interrogating questions about where she'd abandoned the bodies and cars, or how many times she fired her gun. It was hard for her to remember a lot of her facts, because she was always drunk with her clients. She had to be in order for her to perform the sexual acts she didn't really want to perform with them. Being drunk was the way she coped with the lifestyle she lived. She said she was also going through withdrawals during the three-hour long interrogation. She saw worms crawling on the floor, she was distraught and hysterical all at once, so there was no possible way for her to recount all that had happened over that last year.

The world liked to believe that Lee was a remorseless monster. They believed she had not a care in the world for nothing, or no one. When in fact, there was a softer side to her. It's been confirmed several times. Not just by her best friend Dawn, or Tyria, but also bikers from the bars she liked to visit, and it showed in her letters. In one letter she talks about her brother Keith, and how saddened she was when she finally saw how much the cancer had eaten away at his body. She'd hitchhiked all the way from Florida, to San Francisco to visit him at Letterman's Army and Medical Center. She said she got her fare for the trip from a construction worker she met while on the road. He'd given her $100 to make it to see her brother. She used the money to buy gifts for Keith. Stuff she knew he would like. A wooden flute, because he loved to play. She also bought him his favorite book, and a Bible. She remembers finally seeing the tumor on his throat. She said it was the size of a football. When she saw it, she immediately got teary-eyed because she knew that he wouldn't make it much longer. She was also sad after she'd gotten him the flute, because he wouldn't be able to play it due to the seriousness of his throat cancer.

She later found out that Keith had been the hospital's test subject. His tumor started out really small and since he had agreed to participate in some test trials his doctors didn't cut it out. Of course, it grew, and so did Lee's anger when she found out. She charged over to the nurses' station demanding to speak to Keith's doctor and when she finally got the chance to, she really let the doc have a piece of her mind.

Her brother knew exactly how she was making her money. He wanted her to stop doing it, but she insisted she had to. He left her the ten thousand dollars from his life insurance policy in hopes that she would take the money and turn her life around, but life wasn't that simple for Lee. She had a lot of learning and growing to do during that time in her life, and it didn't help that she was losing her brother. She didn't even want to accept the money in the beginning. All she wanted was for her brother to beat his cancer. Her heart was broken when she learned that no one had gone to visit Keith the entire eight months he'd been in the hospital. She even blamed herself for not getting out to see him sooner than she did. She planned on saving up her money and finding an apartment in San Francisco to be closer to him, but after four months of saving, Keith was moved to a different hospital.

Her last letter ever written to Dawn was dated September 26, 2002. In it, she couldn't stop thanking Dawn for all she had done for her in life. Being her friend. Never judging her, even when she'd been judged by the entire nation. Sleeping in cars with her when they were young girls, just to keep each other company. Aileen was actually shocked that Dawn still wanted anything to do with her after hearing about what she'd done. She figured her old friend would have seen the news and wanted to part ways forever, being that she had a husband and children of her own. She talked about how when they both made it to heaven, she was going to show Dawn around just like she had when they were younger. The trips she and Dawn took were always her favorite. She reminisced about the attic parties, the pit and pool parties they threw.

Those were some of the best times in her life. She wished she could go back and relive them once more, before she had to take a seat in the chair of death and face her fate for the crimes she'd committed.

"And buddy—ya left me full of good memories. Even the Mall. I'll never forget that ice cream cone you got with a scoop so hard put on it, that when ya went to lick it, it fell, and went rolling acrost the floor. Boy—that one kept me laughin all day!" she wrote. There were times where Aileen talked about not being able to eat ice cream because she would always start to crack up about that memory with Dawn. Dawn shared the same memories during an interview she had. She wanted to paint the world a different picture of her friend. Something other than the monster they all saw.

Aileen called the snowy nights in Michigan "romantic." That's how deep her mind traveled and no one would ever know had it not been for her letters to Dawn, and Dawn showing up for her friend in her greatest time of need. If Aileen herself had been the only one talking about the good things that come from life and how she saw the world as a beautiful place, no one would have ever believed her. But Dawn made sure the world knew there was more. There was more to Aileen than being a hitch-hiking prostitute. There was more to her than being drunk and angry at the world for the way life treated her. There was more to her than failed relationships and there was most certainly more to her than being a murderer.

She had a good heart beating inside her chest. It showed in the way she took care of people who had less than she had, and she had nothing more than the clothes on her back and the will to survive. She was also smart. She had a particular way with words and always looked at the world, seemingly, through a magnifying glass. In her last letter ever written, she talked about the times she and Dawn would go to Burger King and get whoppers and fish sandwiches. She said they were HUGE back in their day, but as time went on the sandwiches got smaller and smaller. Her answer to that was "Over-population." And it makes sense. In order to feed the world there has to be enough food. Why not change the size, while keeping the price the same? That was the way her mind worked. She wasn't as "dumb" and "uneducated" as the world made her out to be. The majority of what she knew about life came from living life on the road. She wasn't taught in school, like the average adult, her knowledge and education was given to her through experience.

Aileen loved Dawn so much for coming back into her life, she told her she replaced all the love she had for Ty. Coming from her, that was deep. She loved Ty enough to kill for her, just imagine what she would do for Dawn, if she had the chance. She was most thankful for all the good memories that came back with Dawn. It gave her something, other than death, to look forward to. Dawn and her memories helped Aileen prepare herself for the inevitable. In the beginning, she was afraid to die. Even when she was angry and all she wanted was to be put to death. But, when Dawn came back around and showed Aileen that true love never dies, she was more at ease with what she had coming. She felt like she had reached a moment of pure sanity and that her soul would finally be set free from the shackles of society.

Her dying wish was for Dawn to get the truth out to the world about her. She wanted her real story told by the only person she trusted to tell the truth. Wuornos wanted the world to know about the corruption that went on in the police department, the court systems, and the prisons. She also wished she never agreed to sign the movie deal. There are wanderers who wonder if she only regrets signing the deal because she finally found herself in prison and didn't want the truth to be aired, or if there really was some shadiness going on with her lawyers and adopted mother. We may never know the truth behind her accusations, we can only speculate to that. Her letters are very convincing, however, and till this day, Dawn still speaks out in defense of her friend. She never talks about whether she feels Aileen got what she deserved or not, she just tells what she feels makes sense, according to Aileen's letters.

"I'll close here and find a way to relax a little more before the end. I'll see ya at Starke, and again someday on the other side. Love ya buddy, and take good care 'My FRiEND.' You'll be 'FOREVER REMEMBERED BY ME.' Love Aileen." Those were the last words Dawn ever heard from her childhood best friend.

Chapter Ten

In Closing

Richard Mallory was described by one of his employees as "a man who liked women." Essentially, everything about a woman turned him on. Their perfumes and natural odors. Their hair and the style of dress they wore. Everything. He often shared stories about the women he had the pleasure of making love to. He talked about the way he craved the moisture on their skin and how powerful he felt whenever he was with a woman. Sexually. Women were his comfort, and not in the nurturing or sensual way many would think.

Mallory liked to be aggressive with women whenever they had sex. The reason he took so many trips out of town was to meet new and different women. He had his favorite clubs and bars he would go to with the sole purpose of picking up a woman. He was no stranger to paying for what he wanted, party favors, sessions. Whatever term you may prefer. His interaction with women was really the only thing he talked about with his employees. Or anyone. He was a very private man outside of that, an even more paranoid one. His paranoia is suspected to have come from the ten years he spent in prison, for sexual assault.

The people who were around him the most, his employees, felt like he was a mystery. He didn't talk much to anyone he kept employed at his shop; he barely even kept them employed long enough to know their names. That was just how paranoid of a guy he was. John Townsley, a man who worked for Mallory at his repair shop, said that Richard was the type of guy who knew how to get under your skin. If he found you somewhat likeable, you were fine. But, if he didn't like you, that was when he turned the heat up. On purpose. He also said he could never really tell when, or if, Mallory was lying or not. That he told so many stories it was hard to believe what was the truth.

Not many people knew Richard Mallory where he lived. He lived by himself in The Oaks apartment complex in Clearwater, Florida. Not even the complex manager remembered much about the man after he disappeared. It didn't come off as much a surprise to anyone actually. The only thing the super could recall about Mallory when asked, was the number of times he requested the locks on his apartment be changed.

Seven or eight times, he said. And he had only been living there for three years.

When it came time for detectives to look into Mallory's disappearance, their only leads were two phone numbers found in his apartment. The numbers belonged to two strippers that Mallory would often see, before he took his weekend trips to Daytona Beach. One stripper in particular, Chastity, spilled the beans about a date she and a friend were supposed to have with Mallory when he turned up missing. It wasn't unusual for them to go back to his shop and have sex. Sometimes he paid them in cash, other times he would give away TVs and VCRs, that belonged to his customers, for their services. Aileen's reign of terror all stemmed from her encounter with Richard Mallory.

The media liked to believe that Wuornos hated men. Truth is, she hated everyone. There was no discrimination when it came to the wrath of Aileen Wuornos. She had spent more than twenty years of her life working the highways trying to make enough money to take care of herself, and she even helped others around her that she saw were in need. Even though she struggled with her own antisocial and borderline personality disorders.

Her rates were never too extravagant either. $30 for oral. $35 for vaginal sex. $40 for both. $100 to spend a full hour with her. In her younger days, Wuornos was described as a beautiful woman. However, the more time she spent "on the road" as she liked to call it, the more her looks deteriorated. Her blond hair became more stringy and tangled. Her facial expression grew to be more stern and mean-muggish. Not hard to believe, considering how hard of a life she'd lived. She was used to people only wanting two things from her. Sex, and money. That can be something very damaging for any woman.

Munster, lead detective in Marion County, often described her as unattractive. Too aggressive, obnoxious. He even said that a lot of men would send her back to the highway before they even paid her. Every man in Aileen's life had always been a disaster to her. She was molested by her own grandfather. Raped by a friend of his. The boys at her school used her for sex and made fun of her afterwards. Her husband, the man she thought would finally take her off the streets, divorced her after only being married sixty days. It seemed as though her future with any man was null and void. When she finally ran into a man that she actually loved more than anything, even that didn't last. He couldn't deal with her many angry outbursts and quick temper, and left Aileen high and dry.

That yearning feeling that she felt for love left her heart for a while. She didn't want to become emotionally involved with anyone else, her only focus was making money and keeping a roof over her head. And then, she met Tyria Moore. Their connection was instant. And though Tyria dressed like a man most days, she still had the softness of a woman. There was a nurturing aspect to their relationship that Aileen had never experienced before, that was what she fell in love with. As far as society and class goes, Moore's family would be labeled as middle-class. Much more respectable than Aileen, so it was hard for them to be supportive of her relationship with Wuornos. Even Moore wanted Aileen to stop prostituting and get a real job. However, she never turned down her gifts, travels and hotel stays. According to Aileen. However, she loved Moore more than anything. Even more than she loved the boyfriend she nearly took her own life over and spent 18 months in prison trying to impress.

Ever since she was a kid, Aileen had been trying to buy people's love. She yearned so badly for a connection with someone, that wasn't sexual, she would often spend what little money she earned by selling her body to throw parties for the kids in her old neighborhood. But, even that didn't make anyone stick around for too long. They would even kick her out of her own parties because of her obnoxious outbursts, and continue on without her. Not much was different in her relationship with Tyria.

In the beginning, they were solid as a rock. Inseparable, according to the popular Daytona Beach crowd during their time. Aileen was so head over heels for Tyria, she felt the need to take care of her and keep her "kept" the way she was used to living back home with her family. Aileen says that it was Moore's idea for her to start meeting new clients to make more money in the first place. When the money was rolling in and Aileen made enough cash to pay for trips to SeaWorld, and send money to Moore's sister for her to visit, just to make Tyria happy, there was never an issue. It was only when the money ran low and they were back sleeping from pillow to post that Moore put even more pressure on her.

The night she was raped by Richard Mallory, she says, she told Tyria all about it. Moore even helped pack up their things so they could get out of dodge before the police came knocking. When Aileen started downright refusing to have sex with men and just killed them and took their belongings, as well as their cars, Tyria knew about that too. She even drove the car belonging to Peter Siems, and wrecked it. Moore says she begged Aileen to stop being a working girl because it was dangerous work and she didn't want her to end up getting hurt, but on the other hand, she continued to accept the luxuries of Aileen's doing the job. Moore and Wuornos were born into two completely different worlds, so it wasn't a wonder as to why she couldn't see that Moore would turn on her to save herself.

In the end, Wuornos was indeed guilty of her crimes, but were they worthy of death? Did she have a fair trial? Was Tyria really as innocent as she made herself out to be? These were all questions that Aileen asked while incarcerated, and still, no one had answered. She thought she would finally get some answers when Arlene Pralle walked into her life. The 45-year-old "born again Christian" who legally adopted Wuornos, just ten years younger than she was. After Tyria's betrayal, Aileen felt completely defeated. She didn't care what happened to her after that. Arlene claimed to be there to help her through that, in the beginning. However, soon after finding out that Wuornos wouldn't be allowed to reap any benefits from her book and movie deals, things suddenly changed. Pralle's visits to the jail slowed up. The phone calls didn't get accepted as often as they had in the beginning. Arlene's own husband even had words with her over how much debt she was racking up by accepting so many collect calls from the prison. All of that ended after she found out there would be no money coming their way. According to Aileen.

Arlene, of course, told a different story about the ending of their "mother/daughter" relationship. She says that Wuornos became even more angry and hard to deal with. That anger that she tried so hard to suppress, in order to continue belonging in Tyria's life, had come back times ten. She got mean and nasty, demanding money, and even tried to sweet-talk her way back into Arlene's heart once she'd calmed down.

The only relationship that was ever constant in Aileen's life was her friendship with Dawn. The women had gone nearly twenty years without seeing each other, though they always kept in contact by phone calls or letters, and Dawn's views on her friend never changed. Aileen even let her talk to Tyria every once in a while, because she felt like Ty was going to be someone very special to her forever. However, in the end, there was only Dawn in her corner, just like she had always been. Dawn made visits to the prison to see her. She got in contact with her "public pretenders" to keep up with, and also give information about Aileen's life to try and help her case. Dawn was even willing to leave her job in order to be able to take the stand and testify on her best friend's behalf. That was a lot to deal with for a person suffering from MS, but Dawn put herself on the back-burner and kept the promise she had made when they were just teenage girls. She would always be there for her best friend, Aileen Carol Wuornos.

After Aileen's execution, on October 9, 2002, Dawn flew to Florida to pick up Aileen's ashes and bring them home to Michigan. She spread her ashes around the home she built with her husband and children, and even planted a memorial tree for her. She goes out on important days, or when she just needs to feel her friend's presence, and plays the old music they used to like listening to as kids. Till this day, Dawn has never judged Aileen for her crimes. She doesn't even like talking about them. All she likes to remember about Aileen is how big her heart actually was. She often talks about the time Aileen brought her on the road with her. They hitchhiked all the way to California, and Aileen was always mindful of Dawn not being a "working girl," so instead of picking up any johns, she taught her how to pan-handle in order to make money. Those are the kinds of memories Dawn strives to keep alive.

In Loving Memory of,

Aileen Lee Wuornos

February 29, 1956 – October 9, 2002

Made in the USA
Middletown, DE
22 September 2023

39096621R00066